THE
NOBLEST
INVENTION

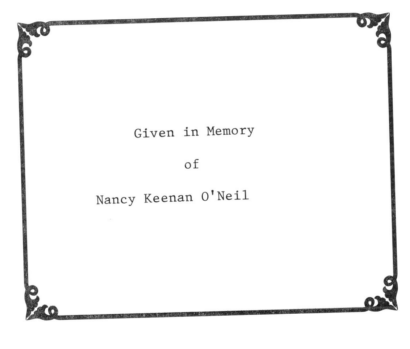

Given in Memory

of

Nancy Keenan O'Neil

THE
NOBLEST
INVENTION

An Illustrated History of the Bicycle

By the Editors of *Bicycling* Magazine

Foreword by Lance Armstrong

RODALE

©2003 by Rodale Inc.
Foreword ©2003 by Lance Armstrong

Photograph and illustration credits are listed on page 313.

Book design by

Library of Congress Cataloging-in-Publication Data
   The noblest invention : an illustrated history of the bicycle / by the
editors of *Bicycling* magazine ; foreword by Lance Armstrong.
      p.   cm.
   Includes index.
   ISBN 1–57954–669–2 hardcover
   1. Bicycles—History.   2. Bicycling—History.   I. Armstrong, Lance.
II. Bicycling magazine.
TL400.N63   2004
629.227'2'09—dc21   2003014227

Distributed to the book trade by St. Martin's Press

2 4 6 8 10 9 7 5 3 hardcover

WE **INSPIRE** AND **ENABLE** PEOPLE TO IMPROVE
THEIR LIVES AND THE WORLD AROUND THEM

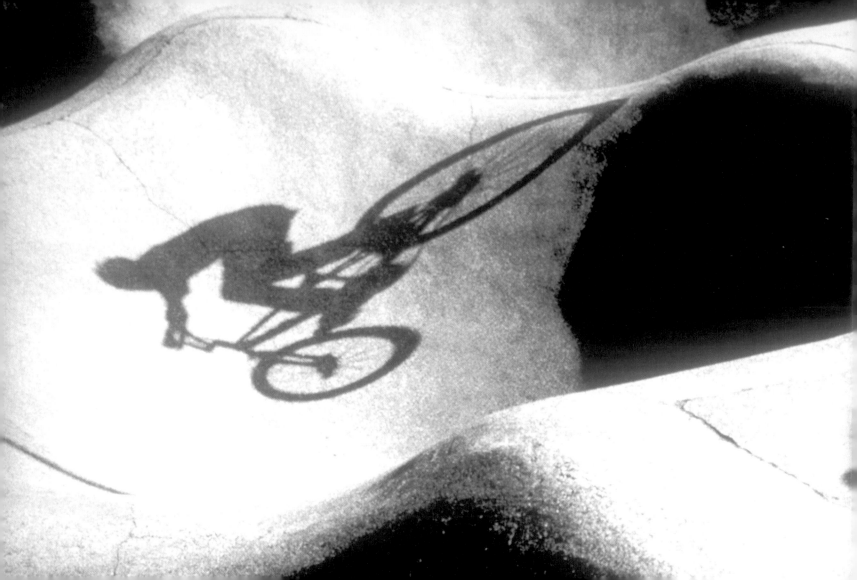

CONTENTS

FOREWORD

By Lance Armstrong

A bicycle is the long-sought-after means of transportation for all of us who have runaway hearts. Our first bike is a matter of curb-jumping, puddle-splashing liberation; it's freedom from supervision, from car pools, and from curfews. It's a merciful release from parental reliance—one's own way to the movies or a friend's house. More plainly, it's the first chance we have to choose our own direction.

A bike is the first wheeled machine we ever steer solely by ourselves, and perhaps for that reason, we have intense affection for and strangely specific memories of the ones we've owned. I myself have had hundreds of them, but they stay with me, like old friends. The physical familiarity you gain with a bike is something you don't feel for any other vehicle, no matter how sweet the ride. My own first bike was a Schwinn Mag Scrambler that I got when I was about seven. It was an ugly brown and yellow contraption, but it was the start of my lifelong attachment to bikes, an attachment that has acquired physical proportions: There are times when I swear a bike is merely an extension of my arms and legs. All these years later, I still have a faint sensation of that first Schwinn, how the rubber handgrips molded to my palms and how the soles of my sneakers grabbed the teeth of the pedals.

My mother, Linda, still has most of the bike parts I've ever owned. The once-shiny components are boxed up and put away; she can't bear to toss them out because they were so hard to come by. When I was a boy, she worked as a secretary, and it was an expensive proposition for her to buy a bike and all the racing parts I wanted. We lived in an apartment in the suburbs of Dallas, across the street from a store called the Richardson Bike Mart. The owner, a guy named Jim Hoyt, had turned it into the headquarters for cycling in the area. Jim knew us from the neighborhood, and he noticed how hard my mother worked and that I was always neat and well behaved. He helped my mother pick out my bikes and gave her deals on them. From then on, the Richardson Bike Mart was where I bought every bike and part I owned over the next decade. That store formed me as a cyclist. I would wander through it staring at the latest gears. I always had a thing for newness, for the latest technology that might result in the smallest increment of speed.

Of course, it's the fastest bikes you remember best. I circled old dirt tracks at Richardson's on a BMX bike. I ran neighborhood stoplights on my first good 10-speed, a beautiful blue Mercier, slim and elegant, that I got when I was 13. Next, I had a top-of-the-line Raleigh with real racing wheels, but I only owned it a short time before I got in a wreck by running a yellow light. I used to like to ride in traffic for the challenge, and one afternoon I whirled through a busy intersection when out of nowhere came a Ford Bronco that hit me straight on. I went flying headfirst through the intersection while metal parts from the totaled bike sprayed all around me.

The last bike of my boyhood was a Schwinn Paramount, which I rode along the black-ribbon rural roads of Texas, dodging pickup trucks as I went for miles through fields as brown as coffee. That Schwinn took me all the way to Moscow—my first trip overseas—for the Junior World Championships. Aboard my current Trek, a fabulous machine of composites so light I can lift it with one hand, I've explored all the different pavements of Europe. I've ridden the bone-jarring and cobblestone-studded coastal roads along the north Atlantic, the winding black-gray routes along the sheared-off cliffs of the Alps, and the parched and jagged approaches to the Pyrenees.

I've been asked many times what keeps me on my bike. How do I explain my desire to ride for hours and even days at a time, up and over mountainsides? The Tour de France is arguably the most grueling sporting event on the face of the earth: We pedal around the circumference of an entire country, over a period of three weeks in wind, rain, and scorching sun, across Alps, through flats, along coastlines, past graveyards and lavender fields, over cobblestones and slick pavement. Why do I do it? The simple answer is that I love to ride.

I ride out of season as passionately as I ride in season. One afternoon I was out on my bike when my cell phone rang. It was David Millar, the great young British cyclist and my friend, calling from Paris. He was out on the town and had a few drinks and decided to give me a ring.

"Please tell me you're not on your bike," he said.

"I'm on my bike."

"No! You bastard! It's December bloody first! How long have you been on it?"

"Three and a half hours."

"No!"

To me, riding is living. When I was sick with cancer, I thought constantly about riding. I daydreamed about the sensations of moving through the countryside on a bike, of the wind against my face. I yearned for the sense of well-being that riding gave me and the pleasant sensation of being spent after a long day. Riding up one of the Alps seemed like heaven compared to lying in a hospital bed drugged, parched, and burned from the inside out. Before, I'd enjoyed riding and the living it provided me, but I hadn't truly appreciated it. After my near-death experience, when I confronted the possibility of never being able to ride again, my feelings for the sport multiplied.

When I was well enough, I'd take short rides around my neighborhood in Austin. Or sometimes I'd go into my garage and turn on loud music, climb on a stationary bike, and pedal furiously until I was covered with sweat. I rode to prove I wasn't dying.

Now I ride to prove that I'm alive. Each time I ride in the Tour, I prove that I survived cancer. I've survived it again, and again, and again, and again. Even in the midst of a hard day on the bike, beneath every pain and stress is the sense of relief and pleasure that I'm able to ride again. I ride to prove that in a scientific and highly mechanized era, the human body is still a marvel.

In cycling, there is no outer skin of metal to protect you from the elements. You have only your flimsy clothing, and this makes it a sport that is as sensuous as it is severe. The cyclist experiences great beauty—sublime views, the swooping exhilaration of a mountain descent—but there's a penalty on the body for cycling, too: A physical toll is taken in exchange for the beauty of the trip to remind you that you are human.

Cycling hurts in a dozen different ways. You're sore constantly. Sore neck, sore knees, sore hamstrings, sore calves. Cyclists get tendonitis all the time. You get it from crashing or from riding in a fixed position for hours on end. You wake up one morning and it's in an elbow or a knee.

But absolutely the worst way to hurt on a bike is to get road rash, the result of your thin skin meeting asphalt and gravel. I've left pieces of myself over all the roads of Europe.

Road rash is what happens when you fall off a bike and skid on asphalt at 40 mph. We're not talking about a scraped knee. We're talking about rolling down crude rocky asphalt of northern France and skinning both sides of your entire body—front and back, too. It leaves you with scabby, nasty, scraped off skin—sometimes to the bone. It hurts. It hurts for days or weeks. It hurts so much you can't sleep. The mere touch of a sheet can make you, rolling over in bed, wake up and groan in the middle of the night, "Ahhhhhh." If you crash and get a bad case of road rash, it could mess you up for the rest of the Tour.

The worst case of road rash I ever had was in the 1995 Tour when I crashed during a stage to Dunkirk. It was high-speed pack finish, and some guy just came up out of nowhere and nailed me from the side. The bike was destroyed, and I went flying across the rough northern French pavement. I had to go to the hospital. I had raw scraped skin all over my body—up and down, left and right. I sat at the dinner table that night, and my friend Fabio Casartelli, the late Olympic champion, said, "No way can you race." I said, "I'll be all right." The next day I didn't see how I'd walk, let alone climb back on my bike. I managed to ride, but gingerly.

But there are also occasions when cycling feels effortless, inhumanly so. My great friend George Hincapie, an American champion and my teammate on the U.S. Postal Service squad, has a saying when he is feeling really good: "No chain." The chain on the bike cranks the wheels and creates the tension in your legs that drives the bike forward. But imagine if you didn't have a chain. You'd spin nothing; air, which would feel real easy. So George and I have this thing:

"Man, can you check something for me?" he'll say.

"What?"

"I don't feel a chain," he'd say. "Is there a chain on my bike?"

It became shorthand, "No chain."

I'd say, "Hey, how good do you feel today, George?"

"No chain, no chain."

I'm awe-inspired by technology that outstrips human performance, and I credit science with saving my life. But a bicycle, no matter how elaborate the technology or how advanced the composite, remains driven by the body. There is something fundamental: a frame with a crank, a chain and two wheels, powered by nothing more than your own legs. On a bike, you are under your own power, directed by your own hand. Your wheel and motor is yourself.

All professional athletes have a relationship with the tools of their sport that transcends familiarity. There was a legend that Ted Williams could see the seams on a fastball. It sounds perfectly legitimate to me. I know scores of stories about how athletes acquire hypersensitivities to the things they use. My friend Tiger Woods is phenomenal with golf clubs; what he's able to do bears no relation to the game of golf, as I know it. It's as though he's got more wires in his body when it comes to swinging a club. On occasion, Nike sends him drivers to test. He can hit a few balls on the range and give you a pretty good guess as to what the specs of the club are. Once, Nike gave him six drivers to choose from, and one was a little heavier than the rest by 2 grams, roughly the weight of a 1-dollar bill. He was able to pick it out without a gauge or scale.

Another time, Tiger was testing golf balls for the different levels of hardness in the dimpled covers. He simply bounced them off the face of his club and could tell by the feel where they ranked, hardest to softest, in perfect order.

I've heard the same types of stories about tennis players. Hand Andre Agassi two rackets, and he'll hand one back to you. "This one's heavier," he'll say.

It's only natural, since I've been on a bike pretty much every day for the last two decades, that I have a sort of heightened sensory sensitivity to bikes. The mechanics on the U.S. Postal Team call me "Mister Millimeter" because I am so particular about the setup of my bike. Raise or lower the seat even a shade, and as soon I'm astride it, I'll say, "Who screwed with my bike?"

Cyclists ask the bike to perform in ways most ordinary riders can't understand much less duplicate, so our equipment is naturally more highly specialized. The manufacturers make bikes and components for Tour riders that are also available to consumers, but it's questionable what percentage of riders should be riding such an elaborate racing rig.

Tour cyclists have higher than average tactile skills; they know how to use a bike in ways other people can't fathom because they're aboard one for so many hours in so many conditions. My bikes are made for the arduous circumstances of the Tour de France, a race so long it's said you have to get a haircut halfway through. I use the same basic model and design that you see in a store, but it's set for high performance racing and also for my own particular physique and riding abilities. Some parts of my equipment are pretty normal, and others are unique and wouldn't benefit any rider but me. There are a thousand small variances from one person's bike to the next, and mine only suit me. People want to talk about the specs of my bikes, but that's really only part of the story. Bikes are like DNA—there are a 100 or more things that have to be matched up in certain ways in order to yield a certain performance, and they're synergistic.

It's hard to say how I arrived at the setup of my bike: I'm very methodical. I tinker, I experiment, and I learn as much as possible: I want to understand a great-looking piece of design and how best to use it. I spend hours in wind tunnels playing with my positioning and testing new components, searching for an extra second here or there on a time-trial bike or a climbing bike. Sometimes it's highly technical stuff, involving power-to-weight ratios, moments of inertia, centers of gravity, the spokes of a wheel, or the shape of a piece of tubing. It goes on and on.

But it's like a sunset—I can't describe how all of the things go together, but I know it when I see it, and, most important, I know it when I feel it. To me, the body will always trump technology.

The British author and cycling enthusiast Graeme Fife wrote of cycling, "Where high performance machines are in competition, their drivers will always have to concede some of their triumph to the machine, or ought to; there are some disagreeable exceptions. But the bicycle can never make so much of a difference that we will call 'Foul' because one rider has a demonstrably, an intrinsically superior machine to another. On the road, at any rate."

In other words, a race-car driver can win a race because he has a better engine or parts or a superior car in general, even if he's not the best driver. But on a bike, all men are equal, with no clear mechanical advantage. It therefore becomes a pure test of endurance and will. The body itself is the more important machine, and whoever has trained it and attuned it most thoroughly—not just his arms and legs but also his mind and heart—will be the victor. That's why a race like the Tour de France is traditionally regarded as not just a contest of speed or endurance, but also a journey or crusade.

We live in a generation of brilliant technologists; we've got a lot of new tools and materials other generations didn't have. But we aren't the first brilliant generation. In 150-odd years of bicycle design and use, the bike has evolved, and certain things have been proven to work. They are as true today as they were 50 years ago. A bicycle is a classic design, and the basic principles on which it works—of power-to-weight ratios and centrifugal force—haven't changed, no matter how computer-modeled and milled the parts are.

The basic concept of a body borne through space freely, with the aid of nothing but a crank, two wheels, and arms and legs, remains poetically unchanged.

What better way to see the world?

CHAPTER 1

WHAT
EVERY KID
WANTS

by Bill Strickland

COMING OF AGE

Every kid's dream:
*a dog, a bike, and an
endless summer day*

One sparkling bright summer day when I was 11, my bike and I ran away from home. I forgot long ago what childish sin I committed but I know that as punishment my bike and I, unbearably, were to be separated for some time.

I'd gotten the off-brand BMX bike as a present only that spring. It had an oval number plate, "pro-authorized" race decals, and crash pads on the crossbar and top tube. The pro-style nubs on the right grip had worn off; my friends and I all rigged our right grips to twist in our hands like motorcycle throttles without sliding off the handlebar. I ran a playing card against the spokes, of course, choosing replacements according to my mood on whatever day the old paper rectangle finally shredded away. (I favored aces and jacks.)

Even with *parents nearby, freedom is close at hand on a bicycle.*

Samuel Beckett *recalled with great fondness that he loved to blow the horn on his bicycle.*

Years later, as a racing cyclist—a "serious" cyclist—I would learn to despise kickstands for their extra weight and aura of geekiness. But on my BMXer, I showcased the kickstand by spray-painting it metallic silver like a tailpipe. The back edge of the seat was curled and crisped; a friend of mine had convinced me that by taping model-rocket engines to the underside of our saddles we could get a burst of speed upon ignition. (All we got were scorched seats, flat tires, severe reprimands from Mom and Dad—and the admiration of every kid in the neighborhood.)

It's not unusual that I can remember every detail of my bike. Esteemed writer Samuel Beckett, describing a bike of his youth, wrote "To describe it at length would be a pleasure. It had a little red horn instead of the bell. To blow this horn was for me a real pleasure, almost a vice."

As a form of expression *or simply as a get-away vehicle— the bike reigns.*

Yet even more vivid than my memory of that bike is how it called to me that day. I'd been riding for about four years but felt myself newly mobile on that big-kid's bicycle—it was never meant to accept training wheels, and it had never known me when I couldn't ride. That was a time when we rode our bikes in packs, kin to the dogs that were also free to roam neighborhoods at will. You rode your bike, dropped it wherever a game started, rode it another block, dropped it, and played more. Your bike was always there. Occasionally a group of kids would go out expressly to "ride" but most often our bikes were not merely a childish game but our accomplices in the entire adventure of being children.

So, picture a day from your childhood, a perfect day—bright, shiny, filled with friends and bikes. Your legs kick. You squint into a headwind of your own creation and gulp at it in greedy joy, like a dog with its head stuck out of a car window. That was my day. The bike rolled with a kind of righteous inevitability; we might go anywhere. My own block disappeared under the rear wheel, then the familiar streets of my neighborhood, then the roads my parents drove. I saw a lake. There were no lakes near our home.

My bike and I stopped. I kickstanded it, left it leaning against itself, wheel turned as if it were watching me, curious.

While I played at the water's edge, someone stole my bike.

The perfect portrait
of childhood:
buddies cruising
the neighborhood

INHERENT OR LEARNED

There is no more useful toy than a bicycle; no vehicle more playful, no piece of exercise equipment so liberating, and no symbol of childhood that so powerfully and paradoxically signals the coming of adulthood.

Your bike takes you down the driveway, over the curb, away from the steady hand of your father, then beyond arm's reach and, eventually, farther. As far as you want to go. The significance is not just the distance that grows between the hand and the bike, but the speed. Even wobbly, unsure, turning to look over your shoulder to see if you truly are riding on your own—even then you are, for the first time in your life, faster than Mom and Dad.

The first *pedal strokes are a timeless rite of passage for any kid.*

GREG LEMOND
The Original American Legend

Back in the dark ages of American cycling, when the United States was considered a Third World country on the Continent where bike riders rule, Greg LeMond was the first to bring the Tour de France to mainstream America and to show Europeans that a cyclist from the States could reign supreme.

Born in 1961, LeMond began racing at age 14 and turned pro by 19. He swiftly established himself among the European elite, becoming the only non-European to win the Tour de France, in 1986 at the tender age of 25.

The next year, LeMond's brother-in-law accidentally shot him during a turkey hunt. Sixty lead pellets penetrated his body, collapsing his right lung, and striking his liver, intestine, diaphragm, kidney, and heart. The following two years were a bleak struggle

marred by poor performances and subsequent health problems as he tried to race once again.

Not ready to quit, he entered the Tour de France in 1989. Although 30 shotgun pellets remained in his body, LeMond was back on top. After more than 2,000 miles, including the towering Pyrenees and Alps, he sat just 50 seconds behind first place. Equipped with aerobars and an aerodynamic helmet (both unheard of in the Tour at that time), LeMond did the impossible: He beat the leader by 8

seconds—averaging an unparalleled 34 miles per hour—in the race's final time trial. The next year, he won once more, icing one of sport's most storied comebacks.

Today, LeMond remains an innovator, lending his expertise to a line of road bikes, stationary trainers, and cycling accessories.

VITAL STATS

NATIONALITY: American

DATE OF BIRTH: June 26, 1961

CAREER VICTORY HIGHLIGHTS: Tour de France: 1986, 1989, 1990; World Champion: 1983, 1989; Dauphiné Libéré: 1983; Coors Classic: 1981, 1985; Tour du Pont: 1992

Keep your will *from wobbling, and your bike will always fly true.*

The bike, the first vehicle we master, teaches us the costs and consequences of propulsion: Fall and you scrape not just your knee but your shiny new machine as well. Forget to inflate your tire and you get a flat. Leave the bike behind the car and it gets mangled.

Some people go so far as to equate the lessons of balance that we must master with, well, lessons of balance. "I finally determined that all failures were from a wobbling will rather than a wobbling wheel," wrote Frances Willard, a turn-of-the-century women's rights activist who learned to ride a bicycle at 50. It could be that when we learn just how much speed will take us around a corner safely, we're learning something about how to manage a career 30 years hence. If so, it is not at all apparent in the moment, and barely there in hindsight, which makes it the best sort of cosmic lesson.

A bike is the one Christmas present every child receives, the birthday gift your parents shouldn't have been able to afford, the unfulfilled dream in the shop window that comes true one time for all of us. A child on a bike is a wish fulfilled and a promise still in the making.

Apparently, *this little one doesn't know there's a lovely bike just over her shoulder.*

"As a kid, I had a dream—I wanted to own my own bicycle," said John Lennon, in *Bicycling* magazine. "When I got the bicycle, I must have been the happiest boy in Liverpool, maybe in the world. I lived for that bike. Most kids left their bikes in the backyard at night. Not me. I insisted on taking mine indoors and the first night I even kept it in my bed."

It's appropriate that our parents give us our first bike, for it's a metaphor of what they must do to raise us: Provide us with the tools we need to leave them. And though the process of learning to ride seems to be almost guaranteed—more of us can ride bikes than swim—it's impossible to overstate the difficulty of what we actually accomplish when we pedal off on our own.

As a child, *John Lennon dreamed of having a bike; doubtful that it was dreamy white and covered with flowers.*

Down the long road
our little troopers go,
soon to return—
for now.

"The machine appears uncomplicated but the theories governing its motion are nightmarish," bicycle physicist Chester Kyle explained to *Bicycling*. "Some things can't be easily defined by physics and mathematics. The interactions of the body, mind, muscles, terrain, gravity, air, and bicycle are so complex that they defy exact mathematical solutions. The feel and handling of a bike borders on art. Like the violin, it's been largely designed by touch, inspiration, and experimentation." *(continued on page 32)*

A bicycle appears uncomplicated, but it's a veritable physics class in motion.

Light Years Ahead of His Time

Born in 1879, Albert Einstein is arguably one of the greatest geniuses who ever lived. His keen observation of the world around him laid the foundation for an explosion of scientific theory. By simply casting his eyes skyward, Einstein dreamed up notions of time and space that forever

Einstein *thought the bicycle was relatively fantastic.*

changed the way we view the universe. And his most acclaimed discovery—the Theory of Relativity—came to him while riding his bike.

While pedaling at night, Einstein observed that the bobbling beam cast from his headlamp always traveled at the same speed, whether he was cruising at a quick clip or coasting to a stop. The theory—that light from a moving source has the same velocity as light from a stationary source—was born on that ride. "I thought of it while riding my bicycle," remains one of Einstein's most renowned quotes.

Another favorite saying—"Life is like riding a bicycle. To keep your balance, you must keep moving"—is indicative of the joyful, compassionate scientist's love of the bicycle. Early in his schooling at Munich University in Germany, he would take bicycle tours with fellow scientists to contemplate the world at large. And during his final years, while at Princeton University during the early 1950s, when the automobile was the mode of transportation du jour, Einstein chose his trusty steed over any other modern engineering marvels. Indeed, the most lasting image of the wild-haired genius is that of him tooling around, atop his bicycle, with his infectious grin, gleefully imagining the next revolutionary idea.

Not only *was riding a bicycle a means of illustrating Einstein's theory but it was also a joyful endeavor he shared with fellow scientists.*

A bicycle is a remarkable feat of engineering—it can carry 10 times its own weight and uses energy more efficiently than a soaring eagle. Yet a seven-year-old can master its mechanics. Indeed, it's the first machine many of us ever take apart and successfully (or not) reassemble. There's something about its lines, some feeling inherent in its circles and curves that appeals to us. Our longing for a shiny new bicycle lives somewhere beyond practical. Toys hit children in waves of popularity and resurgence: Count on the yo-yo to become hot again every decade or so, and hold on to your scooters for the next revival. The bicycle never goes out of fashion. A first bicycle lives in us like a first kiss. A best friend. Our favorite dog.

Riding *allows us to see more of the wondrous outdoors and, most important, to contemplate our place in it.*

Mike Burrows, a designer who's created some of the most stunning modern bicycles, admits: "Some things need to be drawn before they can be designed and understood. Others need to be made first, and the bicycle is the latter," he says. "It is inconceivable that the principles involved in riding a bicycle could ever be theorized first. It's far more likely that the principles of balance related to the bicycle were discovered by someone playing around with things that had wheels. Put simply, a cyclist proceeds in a series of falls that are compensated for by steering the bicycle back under the center of gravity. This complex principle cannot be analyzed by computers but is done automatically by us, clever apes. And it is a skill that once learned is never forgotten."

(continued on page 36)

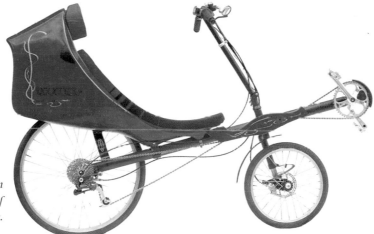

Burrows *believes that the creation of the bicycle was likely the result of a wonderful mistake. We agree.*

"Learn to ride

a bicycle.

You will not regret

it if you live."

MARK TWAIN

LIFE LESSONS

We pine for our lost bicycles. Those that are stolen teach us a whole other lesson about the adult world we're riding so carelessly into. A bike taken is a bike forever elevated in memory. The story is different for the bikes we abandon, which is what happens most often. We leave our bikes as inevitably as we leave our childhood.

I've often wondered if children can sense all that's in a bike, if that sort of ancestral knowledge might explain our intense attraction to these strange vehicles. Is this a modern version of an ordained pairing like caveman and canine? Perhaps the power lies not in the bicycle itself but in the adults who pass on the artifact; maybe we imbue the bicycle with something of what we know. In this way, riding a bicycle is most like crossing a bridge from childhood to adulthood. A kid can pedal across the bridge as often and as far as he or she wants and always return back to being a kid—not so once you drive across that bridge with a car.

Falling *may be the first lesson of riding.*

So strong *is the connection with our bikes that we pine for our lost or damaged bicycles for the rest of our lives.*

The young at heart
can rekindle their
love of bicycling.

As adults, of course, we can cross that bridge, too. Back. Because, if we're very lucky and rediscover cycling when we're older, the bike gets a chance to perform its miracle of liberation again. Just as the bike lets the child glimpse adulthood, so an adult on a bike can sightsee youth. The appeal is not, as it originally was, the magnificence of the distance we can achieve, but the intimacy of the trip. As adults, we might never ride our bikes farther than we drive to work (and certainly few of us ride our bikes farther than we could drive in a single day) but a simple 5-mile spin through the neighborhood can take us much farther than we actually traveled. It's not so much the unknown world that beckons as the freshness of the familiar world you've come to inhabit. You become acquainted with cracks in the road, with curbs, with dogs that confront you. You run your wheels across skittering leaves, drop your head and milk the speed of a fine downhill. Ride a bike through your old neighborhood and you can almost hear your mother calling you in for dinner.

Ride for an hour and you burn enough to enjoy the extra slices of cheese with the wine. Ride through a Saturday afternoon and you no longer have to think twice about that night's triple-fudge sundae—you can indulge as guiltlessly and guilelessly as a child. Ride most of the Sundays through a year and you regain the metabolism of a child, the unthinking ability to incinerate whatever's put in front of you. *(continued on page 45)*

Take the kids *for a spin and reward yourself with a triple-fudge sundae.*

No matter *if the bike is old or new, riding can help your metabolism tick along like that of a child.*

"*Toleration is the greatest gift of the mind it requires the same effort of the brain that it takes to balance oneself on a bicycle.*"

HELEN KELLER

A bicycle moves at the ideal pace to see the world: fast enough to outrace boredom, slow enough to absorb detail. On a bike, you become part of your environment rather than hurtling through it in a car or plane. You can dawdle or blur your eyes with speed and either way be confident that you're moving at a human pace.

Whether *departing on a grand adventure or returning from a short jaunt, riding gets us where we need to go.*

The bicycle is an equalizer; it opens its magic to any of us. Its frame supports people too heavy to even walk or jog; its smooth circular motion soothes damaged knees and welcomes those who can't participate in impact or torsional sports; blind people hop onto the backs of tandems for the thrill of the ride.

Be it in the heart *of Manhattan or on a deserted beach, put two people on bikes and there's bound to be some horseplay.*

Hemingway *was no Sartre, but both loved bikes and the unique perspective they provide.*

Like all aerobic sports, cycling releases endorphins. But there's some evidence that the rhythm of pedaling itself helps the brain mimic the calming and restorative state of deep meditation.

Stephen Crane, Ernest Hemingway, and Pablo Picasso all loved bikes through their lives (and put cycling into their art). Albert Einstein said he thought of the theory of relativity while riding his bike. Simone de Beauvoir told of Jean-Paul Sartre that he "much preferred riding a bicycle to walking. He would amuse himself by sprinting on hills. On level stretches, he pedaled with such indifference that on two or three occasions he landed in ditches."

We never forget how to ride a bike, so the saying goes, and it's so true that it seems an oddity of humanity: Why does this particular machine hold such a spot in our souls? Stop chasing fly balls for a year or two and you're useless in the outfield at the softball game.

Just try to swing among tree limbs like you did when you were seven. But abandon your bike, banish the idea of cycling from your life for 20 years, 30 years, then pick up a bike, throw a leg over it, hop on, and pedal off. It just feels right.

"To ride a bicycle properly is very like a love affair," wrote H. G. Wells in his cycling novel, *The Wheels of Chance*. "Chiefly, it is a matter of faith. Believe you can do it, and the thing is done; doubt, and for the life of you, you cannot." *(continued on page 52)*

H. G. Wells *believed riding a bike was "very like a love affair."*

Party in the Heartland

It started out innocently enough. In 1973, John Karras, the feature writer for the *Des Moines Register* challenged Don Kaul, author of the *Register*'s "Over the Coffee" column to ride his bicycle across Iowa and write columns about the experience. Kaul agreed, with the stipulation that Karras come along. They invited readers to join them, and on August 26, 300 riders set off. Six days later, 114 steadfast cyclists pulled into the final town. In the weeks that followed, the *Register* was flooded with calls from cyclists who missed the event, pleading for an encore. They got it. The second year, 1,700 showed up, and a tradition was born.

On the surface, RAGBRAI (Register's Annual Great Bicycle Ride across Iowa) is like any bicycle tour. Riders start at point A, in this case a town along the Missouri River, and end at point B, which in RAGBRAI is a town along the Mississippi River. What sets it apart is the carnival-like atmosphere. A typical day of RAGBRAI will consist of 60 to 70 miles, with a town stop every 10 to 15 miles. Hosting towns open their bars, set up

John Karras

booths and attractions, and welcome riders to shop, eat, and party. Along the route, there are DJs, music, beer tents, wet T-shirt contests, and raucous festivities. Riders dress

up (or down) in traffic-stopping costumes and often ride together as "teams," such as the Chow Hounds. Some ride the entire stretch; others jump in for a day or two midstate.

Following the *Register*'s lead, more than 40 other states have hosted their own tours, though none has risen to the notoriety of the original. Some 30 years later, RAGBRAI is still rolling strong, with devoted fans signing up a year in advance to ensure their spot in one of the greatest parties on wheels in the United States.

More than 30 years ago, it started as a dare; today it's the best-known multiday bike tour in America.

Then, of course, when it's time for us to pass along the love of cycling, we see the lesson from the other side of the bridge. To run alongside a wobbly but speedy child on a bike is to confront the conundrum of parenting: How much support and how much freedom? In which balance lies success?

Teaching a child *to ride is to confront the central conundrum of parenting: how much support versus how much freedom?*

Faith? Love? Freedom? Is this too much to ascribe to a simple machine on which we are both engine and fuel (as well as passenger and pilot)? Can there be so much that's so elemental in something designed most exquisitely to zoom down hills? The answer is right there, in your bike right now. Put a leg over one, and you can instantly see across that bridge from adult to child. There are about 1.1 billion bicycles making that trip right now. A billion people are pedaling with freedom and joy and innocence on the grandest, noblest toy in all the world.

CHAPTER 2

BICYCLING CULTURE

By Mark Riedy and Joe Lindsey

WHY WE RIDE

Bicycles are the most efficient form of transportation known; they're affordable by almost 90 percent of the world's population and can go almost anywhere, often more quickly, than any other conveyance. But none of that gets to the root of why we spend hundreds, even thousands, of dollars on equipment, why we stare at photographs of beautiful spots to ride, or why we take our bikes thousands of miles merely to ride them in a different place.

Simply put, we ride because we love the ride. The act of riding is at once an elegantly simple and tremendously complex sensation: It is the culmination of hundreds of thoughts and emotions—escape, love of nature, exercise— and at times, the complete *absence* of thought and emotion, a singular focus that allows for no distraction and spares no mental or physical faculty.

The myriad kinds of bikes, and kinds of riders and riding, speak to the multilayered experience that is cycling. It is different things to us all.

A bike ride is *the*
culmination of
hundreds of thoughts
and emotions and at
times the complete
absence of thought
and emotion.

RACING

So enmeshed are bikes and bicycle racing that one can not track the history of the one without tracking the history of the other. For many people, the only contact they have with a bicycle is a clip of the Tour de France on television or a shot of Tour de France champion Lance Armstrong on the cover of national newspapers or sporting magazines.

The first bike race was held in Paris not long after the Michaux brothers became the first to attach pedals to a "bicycle," and today bicycle racing is practiced in every place imaginable—from the urban retreat of Central Park in New York City to the untamed plains of West Africa. In increasingly complicated times, the simple sport of bicycle racing continues to strike a romantic chord in the world's heart.

Bicycle racing *and its timeless brand of escapism has struck a romantic chord with the public since its splashy beginning in the Victorian era.*

TRACK RACING

Due to the lack of good roads and the rudimentary technology used on early bicycles, track racing was the first widely practiced form of competition. As the world entered the 20th century, track racing was the most popular sport, and fittingly it featured the highest-paid athletes. Even in North America, where there were more than 100 indoor and outdoor tracks at the turn of the 20th century, track racing was king. America's first black athlete to be on an integrated team and to be commercially sponsored was a track sprinter of world renown, one Major Taylor.

At the turn of the 20th century, *track racers were the highest-paid athletes in North America.*

MAJOR TAYLOR
Breaking Cultural Barriers

In a sport that is still largely dominated by white men, Marshall W. Taylor was to cycling what Jackie Robinson was to baseball—a brave African American willing to stir up the norm.

Born to a poor rural family near Indianapolis, Indiana, Taylor came into the sport first as an entertainer. Hired by a bike shop at age 13 to perform bicycle stunts in a soldier's uniform, he earned his lifelong nickname, "Major." Four years later, he got his big break, when his boss, well-known bike racer Louis "Birdie" Munger, decided to pull Major out of the stunt-riding circus and put him on the professional circuit.

Despite his speed and determination, Major was plagued early on by racism. Various tracks and championships banned his participation. Then in 1899, at just 19 years of age, he broke through the race barrier by competing in and winning the world 1-mile championship. He went on to dominate the American and European cycling scene, defeating the best cyclists in the world. During the peak of his career, Taylor was earning a dizzying $3,000 a day racing—ranking him among the highest paid athletes of his time.

Sadly, life after track racing proved less kind. Failed business ventures and ailing health sapped his fortune. In 1932, at age 53, he died in a charity ward and was buried in an unmarked grave. Wanting a better end for a forgotten hero, Frank Schwinn, founder of Schwinn Bicycle Company, and other professional racers pitched in to move Taylor's remains to a more prominent grave in Illinois. Today, the Major Taylor Velodrome in Indianapolis is a great lasting monument to his legacy.

VITAL STATS

NATIONALITY: American

DATE OF BIRTH: November 26, 1878

CAREER VICTORY HIGHLIGHTS: 1-Mile Championship: 1899
U.S. Sprint Championship: 1898, 1899, 1900

New York's *Madison Square Garden was originally built to hold Six-Day races.*

The world of track racing and velodromes reached its zenith between 1900 and 1940 when Six-Day racing, where two-rider teams raced multiple events over a number of days, was as big as baseball in the United States. From New York and Boston to Los Angeles and San Francisco, there were major Six-Day events, and lavish stadiums, such as Madison Square Garden, were built to house them. Smoky stadiums in Amsterdam, Moscow, Berlin, Copenhagen, and a dozen or more smaller cities still host successful Six-Day events that are, as ever, heavily wagered upon.

A Multiday Test of Mettle

At the turn of the 19th century, in the glory days of track racing, audiences loved velodrome events so much they couldn't get enough—literally. At Madison Square Garden, track events known as Six-Day races were created to keep the action going. Two-man teams would circle the track for a grueling six days and nights. Before long, these endless sufferfests were the rage across the States and the globe.

Then like all crazes, the Six-Day phenomenon started to cool. Though the rules dictated that only one team member needed to be on the track at any given time, allowing the other to take a fuel or nap break, racers and fans alike grew weary after 144 successive hours. The race format was refined to keep the spirit but also to maintain the excitement. Today's Six-Day races take place over six consecutive evenings instead, so riders and race fans can stay fresh.

Another improvement is that instead of one long race stretching through the night, various miniraces are staged. There are *points races,* where sprinters race for the finish line at the ring of a bell; *miss-and-out elimination races*, where the last rider across the line is pulled from the field, and *motorpaced events*.

At the heart of Six-Day evening events is the Madison. This long, multilap race features team members on the track circling at top speed, while their teammates hover slowly along the boards, waiting until their partner needs a break, at which time they dive down to the field and clasp hands with their teammate, who literally flings them into the ongoing race.

Elements of Six-Day racing are still staples of American track racing. The racing events are popular in Europe, where they are accompanied by weeklong festivities featuring fairs and bands.

The original Six-Day format, *where teams of two riders went for 144 hours straight, didn't allow for much time to rest.*

Track racers differ from other types of cyclists in their raw athleticism. Because there are no hills to climb, track racers focus on building as much muscle mass and power as possible. In fact, the average track racer seems to have more in common with the tight end of a football team than with any other cyclist. With few tracks and little in the way of sponsorship money, track racing remains a cult phenomenon practiced in very distinct locales across the country.

Known as the "race of truth," the Hour Record is the most prestigious title in all of cycling. To claim it, a cyclist must do one deceptively simple thing: Ride a bicycle around a velodrome for one hour, faster than anyone who has ever walked the face of the earth. So elusive is it that only two dozen men have ever held the title in the past 110 years. Among them are giants of the sport:

Urban hipsters *on their way to a coffee house? Nope, they're Cycle Ball players warming up before an indoor match.*

Tour de France founder Henri Desgrange; the greatest Italian cyclist of all time, Fausto Coppi; and five-time Tour de France winner, Eddy Merckx of Belgium.

After smashing the record in 1993, British time-trial specialist Chris Boardman swapped ideas for refined aerodynamic positions and equipment with Scotsman Graeme Obree as both set new high marks. The International Cycling Union (UCI), cycling's governing body, banned the advances and in effect turned the clock back to 1972, reinstating Merckx's 49.432 kilometer record and requiring technologically identical equipment to that used by him for any future attempts. Astride a simple steel bike with no aero wheels or handlebars, Boardman extended Merckx's record by just 10 meters in September 2000. His record of 49.441 km/hour still stands. *(continued on page 72)*

Brit Chris Boardman *has broken the Hour Record on three occasions.*

What Goes Around Comes Around

Soon after men invented the bicycle, they had to decide who was fastest on one—and the velodrome was born. Generally constructed of wood or cement, though sometimes grass and dirt, velodromes are oval tracks used for bicycle racing. They're generally 333.3 meters around and consist of two straights linked with two turns. The turns are steeply banked so riders can dive down off the top of the track at great speeds. Because of the fast pace, photo-finish wins, and propensity for spectacular crashes, velodrome, or track, racing became wildly popular in the States as well as in Europe and Japan in the late 1800s and early 1900s. During the Roaring 20s, nearly every city in America had a velodrome, and indoor racing was one of the nation's most popular, celebrity-packed spectator sports.

But as is the case with all bright stars, track racing eventually lost its luster. The automobile was rolling full speed ahead into America's hearts, and by the late 1940s, virtually all of the hundreds of indoor tracks around the country were torn down. A few outdoor tracks survived the great demolition, but track racing was all but dead in the United States.

Despite what seemed like its final demise, velodrome racing turned the corner and started making a comeback during the late 1950s and early 1960s. The 1970s brought a cycling boom, though there were still only nine world-class velodromes in the nation. Today, in Europe and Japan, thousands of fans flock to velodromes to watch (and often bet on) track-racing events of all kinds. In the States, velodrome popularity is on the upswing once more, with about 20 tracks nationwide and more in the works. With luck, the great sport will rise again.

With no brakes *and four corners per lap, track racing is a thrill-a-second sport.*

For his 1993 record, *Boardman's French-made Corima (above) was absolutely cutting edge.*

CHRIS BOARDMAN
Master Against the Clock

For many racers, the hardest test they face is the time trial. There are no teammates to draft, competitors to chase, or adversaries breathing down your back. It's just you, the clock, and whatever will and power you can muster for the allotted time or distance. Because it exposes riders for their talents alone, cyclists deem it the "race of truth." And Chris Boardman might be the most honest cyclist who ever lived.

Boardman began riding as a teen and quickly qualified to join one of the U.K.'s most prestigious clubs, the Manchester Wheelers. As a young racer, he stacked up 30 national titles and became the man to beat on the U.K. time-trial scene, with only one competitor, Scotland's Graeme Obree, ever nudging him out of the top spot. In 1992, he stamped his mark internationally with a gold medal victory in the 4,000-meter individual pursuit at the Barcelona Olympics.

Throughout the 1990s, Boardman proved he was the fastest man on wheels. He won three Tour de France prologues, clocking the fastest time ever recorded in the 1994 Tour. He captured his first world hour record in 1993; then after a bad crash in 1995, he came back to reclaim the title in a crushing 2000 performance that still stands unbeaten today.

Boardman might still be beating time on his bike were it not for being diagnosed with a brittle-bone disease that forced his retirement. Most agree, however, though the rider has been forced from his bike, his records will likely remain for many years to come.

VITAL STATS

NATIONALITY: British

DATE OF BIRTH: August 26, 1968

CAREER VICTORY HIGHLIGHTS. World Hour Record: 1993, 2000 (still standing); World 4,000-meter pursuit: 1996; Tour de France prologue: 1994 (race record, fastest prologue), 1997, and 1998 Olympic 4,000-meter pursuit: 1992

ROAD RACING

Romantic, tradition-bound, and unmistakably European, bicycle road racing is one of the most dramatic and intricate sports practiced today. The physical demands that it places on the riders as well as the staggering natural beauty of the "stadiums" in which it is played have made road racing one of the most watched sports in the world. Whether it's the highest paved road in the Alps, the thin ribbon of asphalt along the Italian Riviera, a 500-year-old cobblestone path in Belgium's low country, or the diamond-studded Parisian glory of the Champs-Elysees, cycling's drama is acted out on a stage as varied and dramatic as the sport itself.

Lance Armstrong's *U.S. Postal Service Team leads the field in the 2002 Tour de France.*

Centuries, or 100-mile rides, are legion to road riders. There are hundreds of organized century rides, and they've been around as long as the sport itself; no one even has records of who was the first to ride 100 miles at a single clip. But it's a baseline for serious cyclists, a commencement ceremony marking the transition from a person who rides bikes to a cyclist. A century makes sense to people who don't ride; lesser distances don't sound as impressive, and larger ones are a pure abstraction. A century is a universal yardstick for all cyclists and noncyclists alike. Personal physical accomplishments such as riding a century or riding across the entire country, are often compounded by other kinds of satisfaction, such as raising money for a cause.

From its splashy beginning in the Victorian era, road racing in Europe grew in size and stature throughout the 20th century. The grand tours of France, Italy, and Spain blossomed and won a romantic place in the hearts of their nations. Racers such as Italy's Fausto Coppi, France's Jacques Anquetil, Belgium's Eddy Merckx, and Spain's Miguel Indurain became household names and heroes on par with the biggest soccer stars. Beginning with the bike boom of the 1970s and ending with the emergence of mountain biking and triathlons in the middle 1980s, road racing in America experienced incredible popularity among athletes looking for something other than the traditional American sports of baseball, basketball, or football. Yet, from the time of American Greg LeMond's third and final Tour de France victory in 1990 until Lance Armstrong's first Tour victory in 1999, the sport was in decline in the United States, with the spotlight and sponsorship dollars falling to the more trendy off-road events. Lance Armstrong's staggering personal victory over cancer and his five consecutive Tour de France victories between 1999 and 2003 have renewed enthusiasm for road racing and riding across America.

Road racing *epitomizes the drama of the open road with crowds of spectators and hair-splitting turns.*

With fan clubs, corporate endorsement deals, and political influence, today's professional road racers are the rock stars of the cycling world. As riders from non-European nations such as Australia, Columbia, Russia, and South Africa became increasingly competitive, cycling gained a worldwide audience and snared the attention of some of the world's richest companies. Deutsche Telekom, Panasonic, Renault, Peugeot, and Motorola have all given money to appear on the jerseys of the world's biggest cycling stars. Currently Lance Armstrong, the highest-paid cyclist ever, earns more than $10 million per year in endorsements from corporate giants such as Coke, Nike, Subaru, and cancer-drug manufacturer Bristol-Myers Squibb.

Unfortunately, professional cycling will have to overcome the stigma of a sport marred by the use of illegal, performance-enhancing drugs if it is to maintain its global following. In the past five years, a number of champions and several major races, including the 1998 Tour de France, have been marked by illegal doping scandals—dramas that for many fans make the sport every bit as much of a farce as professional wrestling.

American Lance Armstrong *survived cancer to become one of the most dominant Tour de France champions ever.*

CYCLOCROSS

Traditionally a way for road racers to train in the cold, wet winter off-season, cyclocross is part road racing, part mountain biking, and part cross-country running. With its European roots, esoteric equipment, and singular physical challenge, cyclocross has found a committed cult following in North America. At the turn of the century, Daniel Gousseau, a private in the French Army who would ride his safety bicycle on horse paths as a way to stay fit in the winter, began the practice that would evolve into the sport of cyclocross. By 1924 there was an international cyclocross racing scene spearheaded by Gousseau and the French Cycling Union, of which he had ascended to Secretary General. In the 1950s, the sport exploded, crowning its first world champion and extending the international circuit throughout Europe.

European roots,
esoteric equipment,
and a singular
physical challenge
make cyclocross
a cult classic.

Similar to the way that telemark skiing is embraced by those with an overarching need to be different, cyclocross is a splinter of cycling that, thanks to its devoted followers, draws a lot of attention within the cycling community at large. The most tradition-oriented group of racers, cyclocrossers are known for their love of bikes with a foreign accent, vintage wool jerseys, and strong, dark beer.

In cyclocross-mad communities like Boston, Boulder, Seattle, and Santa Cruz, the cyclocross races are as much social outings as athletic events. San Francisco's infamous Team DFL Urban Outlaw Cyclocross-Dress Series has been run since 1996 without permits and rewards racers who aren't afraid to bend their gender by racing in a dress. While not using exactly the same hardware as the cyclocrossers in the United States, the single-speed mountain-bike racing scene that has blossomed around the world is a direct descendant of the cyclocross community's desire for simple technology and difficult riding conditions. Spearheaded by U.K.–based magazine *The Outcast*, single-speed racing has popped up in predictable locales like England, France, and Germany but also in far-removed spots like Finland and Switzerland.

A rider *hefts his bike in a muddy cyclocross contest.*

Freewheeling, *fun, and dirty, mountain-bike racing is a singularly American pursuit.*

MOUNTAIN AND OFF-ROAD RACING

The controversy surrounding the mountain bike's true inventor—was it Gary Fisher, Joe Breeze, a group of Parisians in the 1950s, or even turn-of-the-century off-roaders?—points to the fact that modern mountain biking wasn't so much a technical evolution as a complete social revolution. "We were doing something no one else would. Most Marin County, California, residents didn't go up on Mount Tamalpais, so we had it to ourselves. We did and brought along on the rides things that you would not on a road ride—dogs, full lunch, frisbees, smoke, etc.," said fat-tire pioneer Gary Fisher, of the early days of modern mountain biking.

Unable to assimilate their new culture into cycling's traditional social structure, mountain bikers of the mid to late 1980s created their own vocabulary (*gnarly, shredding, mondo, radical*), dress (baggy, neon, bullet-proof), and currency (scars, tattoos, loud music). They also created their own coronations (the Repack Downhill, the UCI World Championships, and the 24 Hours of Moab) as well as their own houses of worship (Slickrock, Crested Butte, and Mount Tamalpais).

A massive string *of racers shred an alpine descent.*

Mountain-bike pioneer *Gary Fisher rests on the trails of Mount Tamalpais.*

Mountain-bike racing *was first featured as an Olympic discipline at the 1996 games in Atlanta. Here riders start the 2000 Olympic race in Sydney.*

For the most part, it was mountain-bike racing that pushed the fat-tire scene into the spotlight. Led by early champions such as Joe Murray, Ned Overend, Jacquie Phelan, and Juliana Furtado, mountain-bike racing tapped into the public's thirst for adventure and pushed the culture to unimagined heights. The apotheosis of this was in 1996 when cross-country mountain-bike racing was featured at the Olympic Games for the first time ever. The Atlanta Olympics put the mountain bike on display in front of the world, but ever since, cross-country racing and the staid group of athletes that practice it have taken a back seat to more adrenaline-fueled, television-friendly forms of competition such as downhill racing, mountain cross, trials, and slalom. In fact, as mountain biking gained mainstream popularity, many at the sport's core looked for new and original forms of expression. Soon, fringe events like single speed and adventure racing were attracting more and more people.

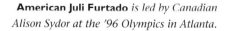

American Juli Furtado *is led by Canadian Alison Sydor at the '96 Olympics in Atlanta.*

FREERIDING

It's hard to say whether the dramatic improvements in mountain-bike technology over the past decade made the freeride movement possible or whether freeriders pushed the technology to accommodate their fast, loose, and out-of-control riding style. The loosely bound, danger-loving freeride scene developed on Vancouver's "North Shore" in the early 1990s and spread throughout the world thanks to the popularity of videos like the *Kranked* series.

Over *dit, ditch, water, or wood, freeriding embraces the virtues of the forest.*

A Mountain-Bike Mecca

Though it's only been around since 1995, Garda Fest, which takes place for four days in the Italian Alps each spring, is firmly established as the single greatest mountain-bike festival on the planet. Chockfull of marathon racing, bike exhibition, stunt riding, music, food, and drink, plus plenty of partying, Garda Fest is a splendid celebration of European mountain-bike culture.

The races alone are spectacles to behold. Created by European mountain-bike event pioneer Uli Stanciu, Garda features three impossibly long race courses ranging from 25 to 62 miles that attract more than 2,000 riders each year. The festival also marks the last stop for the arduous eight-day TransAlp race, another brainchild of Stanciu's. The Garda course itself defines epic. Perched atop towering rock edifices, the trails seemingly snake into the sky. The descents are as

breathtaking as the panoramic views. And the riding is deliciously rough along paths created hundreds of years ago by shepherds, merchants, and military forces. Though the event is in the Alps, which are notorious for cold, wet conditions, the neighboring Lake Garda helps to moderate temperatures for the festival.

Those who don't wish to race can still ride to their heart's content on the stunning mountain-bike trail system. Exhibitors from around the globe show up, offering cyclists an opportunity to test-drive the best new bikes on the market. The area of Garda Trentino has become a magnet for outdoor enthusiasts on and off the bike. For some, the highlight of Garda Fest is simply coming together with a few thousand like-minded people to enjoy the greatest open-air show on earth.

Riding ultrabeefy, full-suspension bikes with between 6 and 10 inches of suspension travel for each wheel and wearing full padding, full-face helmets, and baggy shorts and jerseys, experts in the art of freeriding can shred over, jump off, or huck themselves across nearly any obstacle, whether man-made or natural. As a reflection of their bravado, freeriders tag their trails, cliffs, and gap jumps with grim names such as Lobotomizer 2000, the Spinal Board, and the Wigomatic.

The freeride crowd has traditionally eschewed any type of organization or competition (a favorite saying among the crowd is "bros not pros"), but recently a number of high-profile freeride contests such as the Whistler Air Downhill competition in British Columbia, the Redbull Rampage in Utah, the Red Bull Downtown (run over the streets and staircases) in downtown Lisbon, Portugal, and the Race to the Center of the Earth in Sondershausen, Germany, have gained momentum. Those at the center of the sport wonder whether competition spells the end of freeriding or if it is just a new incarnation.

In freeriding, *there are no obstacles too great to overcome.*

Bike Counterculture

Owing much more to Latino lowrider car culture than to anything with two wheels, the lowrider bike culture is about much more than slammed Schwinn Sting-Rays bedecked with twisted chrome and quilted velour. "A lowrider is more than a bike. It's a culture," says Lilian Robles of the Raza Unida Club in Phoenix, Arizona. "Lowriding is pride which comes from the *corazón* (heart). It is an important part of our Chicano community." With roots in both California car culture and Mexican-American culture, lowrider bikes have their own distinct flavor, flare, and vision.

The preferred platform for even the wildest lowrider bike is a Schwinn Sting-Ray frame from the 1960s and 1970s. Then the two-wheeled lowriders apply the same aesthetic and mechanical language as their four-wheeled familia. Pinstripes of candy-colored paint with glitter, airbrushed fantasy murals, twisted chrome, layers of gold, and even hydraulic shocks and booming sound systems bedeck the two-wheeled lowriders.

An outgrowth of Latino car culture, *lowrider bikes are gold-plated, glitter-encrusted, airbrushed fantasies. Lowrider club members push each other to create more inventive designs.*

ESPN's X Games *has pushed 20-inch riders to new heights and new levels of creativity.*

20-INCH RACING

Action-packed, colorful, and highly individualized, the 20-inch-bike scene started in California in the 1970s as a way for kids to emulate their heroes on motocross motorcycles and has exploded into factions that include flatland riding (once known as freestyle), street-stunt riding, vertical-ramp riding, dirt jumping/trail riding, and standard "old school" BMX racing.

Thanks to the wildly popular ESPN X Games, 20-inch bikes have had a recent resurgence in popularity. Along with the X Games, festivals like the Vans Warped Tour and endless BMX-themed videos and video games feed the desires of the mostly teenage male BMX culture.

Today's BMXers' heroes are legend Dave Mirra, daredevil Mat Hoffman, and speed demons Todd Lyons and Randy Stumpfhauser.

DAVE MIRRA
To the Extreme

Mirra has invented *more new tricks and won more big contests than any other BMX rider competing.*

Known as "Miracle Boy" for his audacious stunt performances, Dave Mirra started competing at 10 and was a sponsored stunt rider by 13. By his high-school graduation, he had gone professional and was considered one of the top ramp riders in the world.

Mirra has earned more medals than anyone in BMX history—12 X Games medals (9 gold and 3 silver) in street and vert (two 12- to 13-foot halfpipe ramps). He was also the first rider to successfully perform a double backflip in competition. *BMX Magazine* named him Freestyler of the Year in 1999, and ESPN deemed him BMX Rider of the Year in 2001.

Mirra has devoted himself not just to competing but also to growing the sport. He started a Woodward Scholarship for kids to spend a week at the famous BMX training facility camp in Pennsylvania.

His likeness is on trading cards, TV commercials, signature bikes, and shoes—even action figures.

VITAL STATS

NATIONALITY: American

DATE OF BIRTH: April 4, 1974

CAREER VICTORY HIGHLIGHTS: Vans Triple Crown: 2001 (3 times) X Games Street: 2000; Gravity Games Vert: 2000; Gravity Games Street: 1999; X Games Street and Vert: 1996, 1997, 1998, 1999

CYCLOTOURISM

The bicycle means different things to a lot of people, but almost universally the bike stands for freedom, and there's no group that embraces the bike-as-freedom concept more than bicycle tourists. Hundreds of thousands of riders log millions of miles every year traveling on every corner of every continent by bicycle.

Tourists range from those who simply strike out on a 25-mile bike-a-thon ride to raise money for a charity to those adventurous souls who load their bikes up with everything they could possibly need for a round-the-world journey. Whether on or off, frequent stops on the cyclotour scene include the olive tree–lined roads of Provence, the golden hills of Tuscany, Holland's endless bike paths, and the spectacular glens of the Scottish Highlands. On the other hand, the Seattle-based International Bicycle Fund (IBF) offers a brand of touring that they consider as much a cultural immersion as a two-wheeled holiday. Those on an IBF tour will have off-the-beaten-path experiences in locales such as Africa, Ecuador, Cuba, and Vietnam and will interact with local people and institutions, learning from their culture instead of simply staying in their hotels and eating in their restaurants.

Cycling vacations in the form of fully supported tours with ride distances between 50 and 120 miles a day, faithful guides, and a comfortable hotel room at day's end are an increasingly popular form of bike touring. Tour operators offer tours that cater strictly to vegetarians and yoga devotees, ones that take you to the highest roads on the earth (both paved and unpaved), ones that follow the Tour de France, and even ones that guide you through the frenzied streets of Paris.

Ernest Hemingway *wasn't wrong when he said, "It is by riding a bicycle that you learn the contours of a country best."*

TANDEMS

Probably the first thing that the Michaux
brothers did after they created their original
boneshaker velocipede was to create a version
of it that they could ride together. "I think
the real appeal of a tandem is that it's
another way for a bike freak to get a two-
wheeled fix. It's also a great way for couples—
where the man is usually faster and more into
riding—to ride together at the same speed
and have the same great cycling experience.
When you're working well together as a team,
an incredible synergy can develop and that's
something that you could never replicate
when riding alone," says tandem designer,
self-confessed tandem freak, and former
owner of Ibis Cycles, Scot Nicol of Santa Rosa,
California. For many, like Will Kelly, a welder
at Eugene, Oregon's Burley Bicycles, a tandem
can be a great way to spend time with his

When you're working well
*together, the intimate synergy of
tandem riding is an experience you
could never match by riding alone.*

kids. "There are parents out there who give up on cycling when they have kids, but for me it opened up a whole new world," says Kelly, of his regular tandem outings with his three grade school–aged kids.

While there are tandem-only races, like the annual Burley Duet Tandem Stage Race in Eugene, Oregon, the road tandem crowd tends to be more active on the touring and century-riding scene. Clubs such as the TROLS (Tandem Riders of Longview, TexaS), CATS (Chicago Area Tandem Society), DATES (Dallas Area Tandem Enthusiasts), and T-BONES (Tandem Bicyclists of New England) organize an endless number of rides, rallies, and tours on any given weekend. The tandem

In the Victorian era, *the tandem was a novel way for two intimates to sneak away from prying eyes.*

as a focal point for social groups extends the world over, with tandem clubs or societies thriving in England, Germany, Switzerland, France, Austria, Belgium, and Australia.

Traditionally for road riding only, tandems have had incredible advances in lightweight frame, suspension, tire, and disc brake designs over the past decade. These improvements have allowed off-road tandems to join the party in a big way. There are a large number of off-road-only tandem rallies and tandem categories at the bigger mountain bike races such as the Sea Otter Classic in Monterey, California, the Leadville Trail 100 in Colorado, and even the 24 Hours of Moab in Utah.

A ride *on a mountain-bike tandem is certain to slap a smile on anyone's face.*

One basic form *of the recumbent is the same today as it was in the mid-20th century.*

RECUMBENTS

Perhaps recumbent riders are unhappy with the traditional bicycle's standing as the most efficient means of transportation in the world (just 35 calories per person per mile as opposed to 1,860 for the average automobile) or maybe they're just people who like to do things their own way—whatever the case, these fanatics are sensible above all. "Recumbent designers may have different ideas on geometry, style, look, and performance, but most know that the bottom line is comfort!" said Bob Bryant, publisher of *Recumbent Cyclist News.*

Recumbent bikes and their devotees have always been treated as outsiders by the main cycling community. When the recumbent bike—defined as any bicycle that you ride in a prone position—was banned by the UCI in 1934 after an early recumbent design was used to smash many world records, recumbent riders were forced to create their own clubs, events, and organizing body, the International Human Powered Vehicle Association.

Through the middle of the 20th century, the recumbent world was a very quiet and lonely place to be, but in the early 1980s, when the E. I. Dupont company offered $15,000 to the first human-powered machine that could break 65 miles per hour, the cult of the recumbent regenerated. Today you can find recumbent-centric clubs and groups in nearly every state and a number of countries worldwide, including France, Belgium, Holland, England, and Australia.

An upright position, *comfortable saddle, wind fairing, and steady handling geometry on recumbent bikes define cycling sensibility.*

CHARITY RIDES

Organized rides satisfy many needs and wants for cyclists—community, camaraderie, challenge, a sense of purpose, and the chance for social activism. Charity rides comprise the single largest rides in the country. Donors support riders to ride a distance, say, from San Francisco to Los Angeles, and the money goes to a charity.

The oldest continually run charity rides are the MS Bike Tours, a benefit for the Multiple Sclerosis Society, which date to 1979. Various rides around North America, including the 80 different MS Bike Tours, raise money for all manner of diseases and illnesses—from diabetes to cancer. But no phenomenon quite energized the riding, and charity, communities like the AIDS Rides.

The AIDS/LifeCycle *ride from San Francisco to Los Angeles* (left) *raises in excess of $4 million dollars per year. There are more than 80 MS Bike Tours* (right) *every year.*

The original AIDS Ride went from San Francisco to Los Angeles in 1994. It was an instant smash success. AIDS awareness was beginning to take hold; the disease had broken its stereotype as a "gay man's sickness." The HIV-positive included people from all walks of life, including many who contracted it not through lifestyle choices but through blood transfusions and other tragic mishaps. Now billed as "The AIDS/LifeCycle," the 585-mile ride from San Francisco to Los Angeles attracts more than 900 riders and raises in excess of $4 million dollars for the San Francisco AIDS Foundation and the L.A. Gay and Lesbian Center every June. The format has been copied around the country, and now multiday tours that benefit HIV/AIDS research or charities are held every summer across the United States. As AIDS became the biggest worldwide medical issue in the 1990s, eclipsing even bigger threats like heart disease and cancer, the AIDS Rides grew. Thousands of people—many of them complete cycling novices who had never done more than 20 miles on a bike—were riding hundreds of miles in five, six, and seven days to raise millions of dollars for research for a cure.

If the effect on the research community was huge, it had no less impact on the riders, many of whom were attracted to the rides because of friends and loved ones lost to the devastating effects of AIDS. Crossing finish lines in countless cities across the country, grown men and women collapsed and cried, not from pain or exhaustion, but from overpowering emotion—the feeling that in the face of a faceless killer that could not be stopped, they were doing *something*, that somehow they were helping.

Riders celebrate *their accomplishment, a tradition since the first AIDS ride in 1994.*

A TOOL IN THE WORKPLACE

There may always be hot debate about who actually invented the bike, whether it was the French, the English, or even the Chinese, but one thing is for sure: Long before it was raced over the roads of France and in the mountains of Colorado, the bike was used as a tool in the workplaces of the world.

Once the industrial revolution was in full swing, the bike-as-tool was a common sight and it wasn't until the automobile reached critical mass that the bike was outdone for convenience and utility.

The Tour de France *would be a cakewalk for this gentleman.*

The original Postal Service *cycling team, wool uniforms and all*

A Nation on Wheels

The simple, unadorned bicycle is a symbol as evocative of China as the Great Wall itself. There are close to twice as many bikes in China—540 million—as people living in the United States. For decades, the "steel horse" has been the primary means of transportation for the average Chinese citizen to negotiate dusty city streets en route to work, run errands, and attend leisure activities. Unlike the great serpentine barrier, the bicycle may soon all but recede from view in a nation where it once ruled.

China's love affair with bicycles began in the late 1800s, when Americans Thomas Gaskell Allen Jr. and William Lewis Sachtleben spent two years pedaling the 7,000 miles from Constantinople to Peking. Villagers met them with enthusiastic fervor, and before long, Chinese royalty had taken a fancy to two-wheeling around their palace

grounds. Following the 1949 Communist Revolution, a mass bicycle movement emerged, when the government encouraged—and actually subsidized—families to purchase bicycles. As China opened up economically during the decades that followed, bike ownership soared.

Today, a rapidly growing number of citizens are interested in "upgrading" their two-

wheeled vehicles to the four-wheeled variety. Automobiles are the new status symbol in a nation hopeful to modernize—a development that is causing unprecedented traffic snarls. As pollution and traffic jams increase, trips via bicycle have fallen dramatically. The one-time bicycle epicenter of Shanghai has plans to force bicycles out of the center city by 2010.

MESSENGERS

Facing danger, catastrophe, and contempt down every avenue, the life of a bike messenger is one of absolute extremes. Often underpaid and always underinsured, bike messengers are a tight-knit group that, while even in fierce competition for the most lucrative runs, maintains an intense loyalty to their brotherhood. The generally poor working conditions and knowledge that tomorrow could be their last day, have led to the formation of a number of umbrella groups or associations that give the independent messengers some collective leverage when it comes to bargaining for wages, purchasing health care, or finding a new bike.

With a cab *and a messenger in quarters this close, an altercation is sure to follow.*

Perhaps looking to recreate the thrill of their hours on the clock, messengers are increasingly using their off-hours for bike-oriented events from weekly rides and weekend tours to illegal Alleycat races. Every year the messengers of the world select an urban setting for the Cycle Messenger World Championships. Proof of the global reach of the two-wheeled messenger, the Messenger World Championships have recently been held in Seattle, Copenhagen, Budapest, Zurich, Barcelona, and Toronto. Partly a race, definitely a party, the Messenger World Championships event is hard to beat when it comes to fun and freakishness.

Whether it's to document their colorful lifestyle or simply to find an outlet for their challenging existence, messengers express themselves through an incredible number of magazines, Web sites, and art shows.

A trio of messengers *duke it out at the annual Cycle Messenger World Championships.*

MOUNTED POLICE

Detroit, Michigan, was one of the first cities
in the United States to employ the bicycle
in the fight against crime when, in 1897,
expert cyclists called Scorchers were expressly
employed to apprehend speeding cyclists in
the premotor city.

Sadly, the rise of the auto as a crime-
fighting tool in the 1920s and 1930s went
hand in hand with elimination of the bike (and
the rise in the average size of police uniform
pants). But, in 1987, after the Seattle police
department saw a drop in their effectiveness
due to extraordinary traffic congestion
that resulted from a major downtown
refurbishment project, they returned to
the bike as a basic, but effective cruiser.

An early company *of Scorchers*
muster for inspection.

Police *mounted on bikes can get into tight places faster than in cars.*

Championed by energetic officers looking to step away from their cars and backed up by the relative cost (a patrol bike costs just $1,200 to purchase and $200 to maintain annually while it's $23,000 to $28,000 to purchase a new patrol car and $3,000 to $4,000 to maintain it), bike patrols sprung up across the nation. Today, the International Police Mountain Bike Association counts more than 2,000 different mounted units amongst its ranks.

Seattle police *stand at the ready at a protest in 1987.*

Cycle-mounted military units *were used in 20th-century conflicts.*

ARMY

While an Army may travel on its stomach, the world's fighting men and women have, since the bicycle's invention in the 19th century, managed to make great use of the bike. The Chinese army is said to have used a rudimentary *walking machine* to send messages between troop formations as early as 1810. Later in the 19th century, England, France, and Switzerland among others had complete bicycle-mounted corps; in fact, Switzerland maintained a large bicycle-mounted unit until very recently.

The 25th Infantry Bicycle Corps, a unit of the Buffalo Soldiers, were America's first bicycle-mounted unit and were noteworthy both for their mode of transportation and because they were all of African-American descent. In a legendary escapade in 1897, the 25th, looking to demonstrate the bicycle's effectiveness as a troop transport, rode 1,900 miles from their base in Montana to Saint Louis, Missouri. As a reward for their ingenuity, the Buffalo Soldiers of the 25th were sent to Cuba to keep peace in Havana in the wake of the Spanish-American war.

The bicycle maintained its popularity through both world wars, but especially in World War II, where entire units of specially trained paratroopers were dropped into battle with custom folding bicycles strapped to their packs. In recent years, advances in bike technology have again given the bicycle currency with the world's armed forces.

A **detachment** *of the Belgian Congo Cyclist Company in World War II, with their steeds*

Symbol of a Rising Nation

Fausto Coppi may not be the greatest cyclist who ever lived, but he accomplished one of the greatest feats an athlete can—elevating his countrymen during their darkest hours. As an army infantryman in Tortona, Coppi rose to cycling prominence during the 1940s and 1950s, right as Italy was recovering from a devastating World War and years spent toiling under a terrible dictatorship. As the unofficial ambassador of the nation, the *Campionissimo* (the Great Champion) represented a population that could come back.

Coppi was easily the best time trialist of his time and could climb, as Phil Liggett would say, like a "homesick angel." So electrifying were his performances in the mountains that he won the 1952 Tour de France by a stunning 29 minutes and wasn't invited back the following year for fear that he would dominate again. His duels with arch rival and fellow Italian Gino Bartali are legendary.

Equally legendary is how Coppi met his demise. A series of unfortunate events including his brother's death in a crash in 1951 and an illicit love affair with a married woman (he, too, was married) in 1953 deterred from his performance. Then in 1959, during a trip to Africa for a criterium, Coppi caught malaria. The disease was misdiagnosed, and he died in Italy at age 40. More than 40 years later, Italian prosecutors reopened the case, claiming they had evidence that the great Coppi had actually been poisoned by a foe in Africa. The allegations have been largely dismissed, but the Italian legend's death will always be a mystery.

VITAL STATS

NATIONALITY: Italian

DATE OF BIRTH: September 15, 1919

CAREER VICTORY HIGHLIGHTS: Tour de France: 1949, 1952; Giro d'Italia: 1940, 1947, 1949, 1952, 1953; Milan–San Remo: 1946, 1948, 1949; Paris–Roubaix: 1950; World Hour Record: 1942

BIKE ADVOCATES

With a dream of making their cities and streets more livable and safe, bicycle advocates fight to make the bike a broadly accepted mode of everyday transportation.

On the last Friday of September in 1992, bike advocates staged their most high-profile, high-impact escapade, gathering en masse in the streets of San Francisco at the height of Friday's rush hour in order to demonstrate the very real effect that the bicycle can have on traffic. Led by Chris Carlsson and a few friends, the group spun the mantra "We're not blocking traffic, we are traffic," into a monthly traffic jam and a radical mission to give "bicyclists of all persuasions the chance to see that we are not alone, and that we, too, have a right to the road."

Chris Carlsson (right) *and colleague Jim Swanson make bicyclists aware of their rights on the road.*

A decade after that first spontaneous meeting on San Francisco's Market Street, the Critical Mass movement has pushed successfully for bike lanes, bike racks on buses, car-free zones, and improved mass transit in dozens of cities in the world.

Long before there were such things as traffic jams or smog alerts, there was the League of American Bicyclists (LAB). Started in 1880 as the League of American Wheelman, the LAB has served as a unified voice for cyclists' rights and desires for 123 years. Whether a proponent for improved roads that ultimately led to the first mile of U.S. paved road, an information clearing house for enthusiastic bike tourists during the 1970s touring boom, or an advocate for cyclists injured in road-rage incidents, the LAB is the most high-profile friend of the world's 41.4 million cyclists.

The popularity of the high-wheeler peaked in 1880, but enthusiasts still abound.

CHAPTER 3

HISTORY

By Joe Lindsey

MAN-MADE MACHINE

The inventions that change the world are often those that carry the most sublime versatility, a seamless transfer from one use to the next. The bicycle is one such invention. It is simultaneously transportation, recreation, freedom, and mobility.

Bicycles are used to haul goods, to expand the range of a serviceman, to travel long distances quickly and efficiently, and to open new opportunities. Bicycles are affordable to most of the world's population; for many, they are their primary transportation after walking. Bikes are cheaper to own than horses or cars, easier to store, and more efficient per mile than any form of transportation ever invented. And they've captivated our imaginations for centuries. *(continued on page 127)*

Sublimely versatile: *The bicycle is simultaneously transportation, recreation, freedom, and mobility.*

A mid-20th-century *freerider*

Workers in Asia *give a first-hand lesson on the practicality and cost-effectiveness of the bicycle.*

Army cadets *at Sandhurst receive physical training, around 1925.*

The first known drawing of a bicycle-like machine can be found in Leonardo da Vinci's *Codex Atlanticus*, a notebook of scribbles, notes, and drawings that dates from around 1493 (and which also featured a drawing resembling a hang glider). While the actual bicycle drawing is thought to have come from an apprentice of his, da Vinci also sketched a chain-and-cog drive train and even ball bearings in other notebooks, inventions that would not surface for more than 400 years later but would have immense impact not only on the bicycle but also on the dawn of the Industrial Revolution. Another pre-bicycle drawing, "Witches," by the Dutch Renaissance artist Hieronymus Bosch, features what looks like a primitive unicycle.

This early bicycle-like device *was originally thought to have been drawn by Leonardo da Vinci.*

Two-wheeled devices that rolled under human power wouldn't really come into existence until the early 18th century. The earliest known is the *Laufmaschine* (running machine), also known as the Draisienne (after its inventor) or the swiftwalker, which was first demonstrated in August 1817. It was certainly primitive—a wooden beam set between two wheels—but it had a steering mechanism and a seat and looked, actually, not too far removed from a modern recumbent bike.

The Laufmaschine was an intriguing invention, but its central limitation was its speed under human power. Inventor Karl von Drais claimed in his patent application that on level ground the machine was capable of going 9 miles an hour; faster than walking to be sure, but far below even a tourist's pace on a modern bike today. The problem was drive—you pushed off the ground on the

Von Drais' Laufmaschine *was all the rage in Paris in 1817.*

Von Drais *patented later renditions of the early swiftwalker or Draisienne.*

The Pedaler's Perch

Throughout history, the bicycle seat has taken quite a bum rap. Sore-bottomed critics have blamed the humble saddle for everything from boils to impotence. The quest for a more comfortable ride has led inventors to concoct saddles resembling a toilet seat or a hammock, but eventually they settled on the popular bike seat of today—an amalgamation of the rest.

Possibly recognizing the need to relieve pressure on delicate nether-region tissues, early saddles of the late 1800s were part donut, part commode. The popular Bunker Pneumatic design of 1892 resembled a modern comfort saddle, except that it was hollowed out in the region of the buttock and crotch. The Safety Poise Pneumatic of 1898 was less saddle and more shaped like an inner tube, providing only a circle of support to sit on. Tinkerers of the time continued adjusting the design, at one point developing a split saddle that allowed each half to move independently as the rider pedaled. In 1966,

In the past 150 years, *saddles have progressed from early torture devices to ultracomfortable gel-injected seats.*

inventor Dan Henry got the notion to simply attach an upside-down set of drop bars where the saddle should be, sling fabric between the two bar ends and make a riding hammock— likely comfortable for sitting, but not too safe for riding.

The saddle craze settled down soon after that, with most seats resembling the classic bike-seat shape we know today: long, slender nose and flared back. Then in the mid-1990s, controversy rolled into the saddle industry again, this time on the back of some well-publicized research that bike seats caused impotency. Offended racers paraded out their children as proof of their potency, but the bike industry quickly designed "anatomically correct" saddles with small grooves or cut outs in the nose to relieve unwanted pressure. So the story ends—for now.

Laufmaschine rather than pedaling, and so at 9 miles an hour, the rider couldn't get any more purchase—it was terminal velocity. Two Scotsmen, Kirkpatrick MacMillan and Gavin Dalzell, working separately but nearly simultaneously, are credited with adding mechanical drive to the *velocipede,* as the early bicycle was called. Hand and foot treadle cranks were both tried, with some limited success; MacMillan never patented his invention, nor did it ever go into production.

The beginnings of the real bicycle, that pedal-driven invention we are familiar with—from the quaint solid-rubber-tired high-wheeler to the modern downhill bike with 9 inches of suspension travel and hydraulic disc brakes—had to wait until the 1860s.

EVOLUTION OF THE BICYCLE

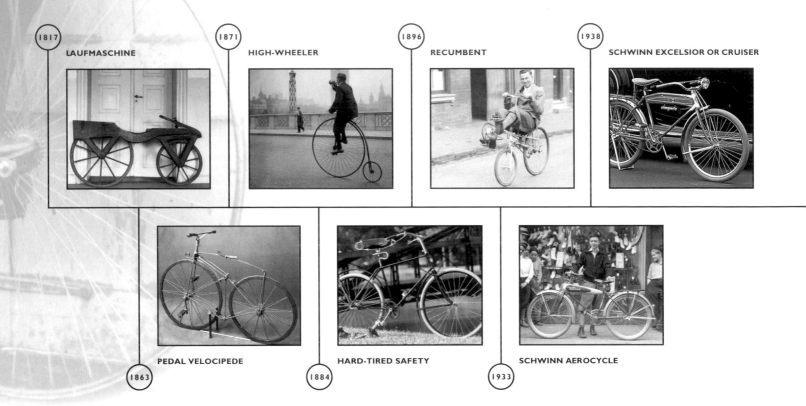

1817 LAUFMASCHINE

1871 HIGH-WHEELER

1896 RECUMBENT

1938 SCHWINN EXCELSIOR OR CRUISER

1863 PEDAL VELOCIPEDE

1884 HARD-TIRED SAFETY

1933 SCHWINN AEROCYCLE

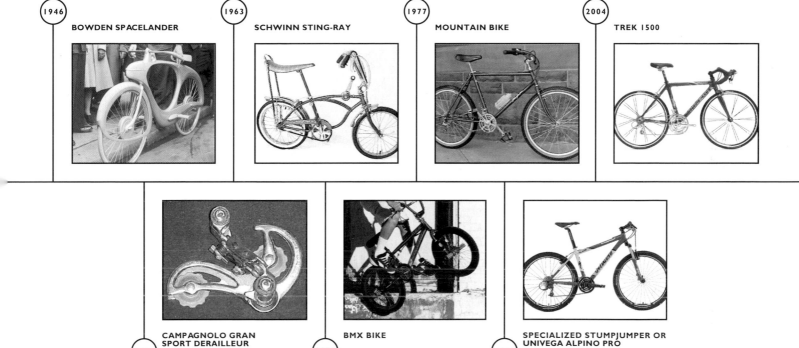

1946 BOWDEN SPACELANDER

1963 SCHWINN STING-RAY

1977 MOUNTAIN BIKE

2004 TREK 1500

1951 CAMPAGNOLO GRAN SPORT DERAILLEUR

1970 BMX BIKE

1982 SPECIALIZED STUMPJUMPER OR UNIVEGA ALPINO PRO

Hell of the North

The beauty of Paris to Roubaix is that it exists. Most agree that a race so treacherous couldn't be designed today. After all, what pro roadie would want to risk bent wheels and broken limbs in the dangerous inferno of crashes that plague a race so wicked that it's been deemed the "hell of the North"? Yet nearly 200 of the top riders in the world show up each year for this grueling century-old challenge.

Originally designed in 1896 as a warm-up for the Bordeaux to Paris race, Paris to Roubaix has developed a fervent following among racers and fans alike. Also known as the "Queen of the Classics," the course snakes

The Queen of the Classics, *Paris to Roubaix is as gritty and demanding today as it was in the 1960s.*

170 miles through the narrow, rough roads from Paris to Roubaix. What sets it apart from other single-day European classics are the legendary 20 to 30 sections of *pavé*, large, irregular cobblestone-like rock stretches that pummel what little energy is left out of already weary racers. As if the merciless terrain were not enough, Paris to Roubaix is equally notorious for its impossible racing conditions. Held close to Easter each year, the weather tends to be rainy and damp, making negotiating the pavé sections akin to biking on ice. Dry weather is little better, as hundreds of wheels kick up dark brown clouds of choking dust. Through the years, as more pavé roads have become paved roads, the race has been rerouted to maintain its rugged difficulty.

The result: No race beside the Tour de France boasts such an illustrious list of victors, including Fausto Coppi, Eddy Merckx, and Bernard Hinault. Often, there is one lone rider who survives the cobbles and pulls into the Roubaix velodrome for a victory lap well ahead of his fellow contenders, basking in some well-deserved limelight. Ever since its inception, a win in Roubaix is truly a badge of honor.

Bumping along *the* pavé *is par for the course during this 170-mile challenge.*

BIRTH OF THE BICYCLE

Like many inventions—the TV, for example—the bicycle's true inventor is somewhat up for debate, and the inventions that popularized it—pneumatic tires, gear differentials, and suspension—were the contributions of many different people.

The father-son team of Pierre and Ernest Michaux are commonly credited with "inventing" the bicycle in 1864 at their Parisian carriage shop. It's unknown which member of the Michaux clan had the idea to put pedal cranks on a velocipede, but the invention was a quantum leap for the nascent bicycle. Quantum in the physics sense: There was no historical basis for a pedal crank for propulsion; the idea was truly original.

Historians will argue *forever over the identity of the true inventor of the bicycle.*

Why is a pedal crank so significant? A treadle crank, in which a lever arm is drawn back and forth like an oar to create torque, is limited by the rate of that back-and-forth motion; you can only row so fast. But pedal cranks spin in a circle, meaning that the pedaler never has to reverse the momentum at the end of the power stroke; power is also delivered more consistently (leveling out the peaks and dead spots in a treadle stroke) and rapidly, allowing average speeds that dwarfed the top speed of the swiftwalker or a treadle-crank machine.

Attaching a lever *arm directly to a wheel completed the basic structure of the bicycle.*

Also laying some claim to the bicycle's invention was Pierre Lallement, who holds the first known patent on a bicycle, dated November 20, 1866. Lallement had worked for the Michauxs around 1865 but claimed in his patent that his invention dated from an idea he'd had in 1862 and that he'd built his first bicycle, or pedal velocipede, as they were then known, in 1863.

Pierre Lallement, *who was hired by the Michauxs in 1865, has the first-known patent for a bicycle—dated 1863.*

Lallement's patent was not only the first bicycle patent, but it was also an American patent, one that changed hands several times. The fight over royalties and the subsequent consolidation of the bicycle industry were parts of the zeitgeist that ushered in the Gilded Age; at one point, the monolithic American Bicycle Company (ABC), the largest bicycle maker in the United States, which had bought out many of its competitors, had John D. Rockefeller as one of its controlling partners.

Inventions like *the bicycle fueled the industry and politics that mark the Fin-de-Siècle Gilded Age.*

This early rail bike *could be pedaled and cranked anywhere there were tracks.*

Whimsy and innovation *are common themes in early-20th-century Art Nouveau bicycle advertisements.*

Innovation was synonymous with *bicycle* in the late 1800s, due partly to the aggressively enforced patent restrictions of the ABC. Many of the best innovations were not specific to the bicycle itself; they did, however, revolutionize what a bicycle was capable of. The most impressive ones are ball bearings, the chain drive, and the pneumatic tire.

It's hard to overstate the importance of the invention of ball bearings. In his encyclopedia of human-powered transport, *Bike Cult*, author David Perry memorably calls them "the atoms of the machine age." Patented by E. A. Cowper in the 1860s, metal roller and ball bearings replaced primitive and temperamental sleeve bushings made of materials such as leather and wood. The incredible decrease in friction allowed longer durability of any wheeled contrivance, whether a bicycle or industrial implement.

A wise husband *will always give his mother-in-law the best bike.*

As much as friction and durability of the hub parts, the central problem of a high-wheel bicycle at the time was its direct drive; the only way to get a higher gear was to build a larger wheel. High-wheelers of the late 1800s had front wheels ranging from 50 to 60 inches in diameter—nearly 5 feet tall. The rider was perched on a simple serpentine-style frame bar above the front wheel—a precarious position given the twitchy handling and bumpy ride.

Nineteenth-century *high-wheeler–mounted deliverymen enjoy a respite from their rounds.*

Racing only his shadow, *a man in knickers demonstrates his high-wheeler daring.*

And gear size was somewhat limited by rider size (the rider's inseam had to be at least half that of the wheel diameter or he couldn't reach the pedals). Braking was dangerous at best—an arm-driven lever was depressed on the front tire—but the so-called spoon brake did little to slow the bike, nor would you want it to be especially powerful or an over-the-bars trip might ensue. Riders more commonly slowed the bike by applying back pressure on the pedals.

A dapper dandy *on an incredibly ornate Michaux-era boneshaker velocipede*

Cycle racing *in its earliest form, probably from the 1870s*

High-wheelers, *roughly the height of horses, had an obvious advantage here.*

Various high-wheel makers experimented with chain drives; the earliest we know of is Ernest Meyer and Andre Guilmet's chain-and-cog system in 1868; their invention never took hold, though, and it was up to later cycle makers such as Thomas Humber, who first adapted chain-and-cog setups from machinery to bicycle use.

Even with such proclivities, high-wheel bicycles were still preferable to "safeties," bicycles with more or less equal-size wheels, because of one additional factor that ranks above raw speed: comfort.

This **safety** (left) *has variable gearing. An early safety* (right) *is being carefully inspected.*

After nearly *half a century of experimentation, the modern safety bicycle became what we know today as a bicycle.*

The solid rubber tires then available afforded a harsh and bumpy ride, and the larger wheels of the so-called ordinaries were more adept at absorbing impact through the spokes. This became particularly true when James Starley pioneered the use of tangentially spoked wheels where the spokes leave the hub at an angle and cross over other spokes. The design, first used in the 1880s, was so good that it is still the primary spoke pattern today. Starley, a prescient man with a gift for engineering, also gave us hollow frame tubing and an invention that would eventually find its greatest use in the car: differential gears allowing two wheels on the same axle to turn at different rates. The differential is the basis for controlling any vehicle with multitrack wheels.

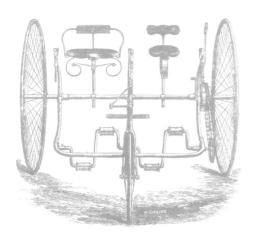

Owners *of these high-wheelers* (right) *stand proudly with their bikes, around 1890.*
James Starley *built this side-by-side "sociable" cycle* (left) *and his shop perfected the early safety bicycle.*

But another innovation vied for the unofficial title of most wide-reaching: the pneumatic tire. In 1888, John Boyd Dunlop, a Scottish veterinarian, living in Belfast, Northern Ireland, was trying to give his son's tricycle a smoother ride when he hit upon the idea of using air to cushion the ride. He took thin sheets of rubber and wrapped them around the wheels, gluing them together to form a continuous layer, and inflated them with a soccer ball pump. Intuitively sensing the impact of his then-crude invention, Dunlop applied for a patent later that year.

The tires were an instant hit, were sold in most of the Western world by the turn of the century, and instantly revolutionized bike design by making the ride more comfortable. Bikes with smaller wheels could now roll over many obstacles. The ride wasn't so harsh as to merit the derisive nickname "boneshaker," which had been given to early velocipedes; when the tires were combined with the chain-driven drivetrain, safety bikes became an obvious choice over high-wheel models.

A side effect of the pneumatic tire was the creation of better brakes—the weak spoon-lever type brake didn't work as well on pneumatic tires. The higher speeds made capable by air-filled tires also necessitated stronger brakes, which resulted in the first coaster-brake hub (the New Departure, in 1898) and the caliper rim brakes we know today. Dunlop's invention also spurred the first freewheel, which was introduced in 1897 and allowed riders to coast at speeds faster than they could pedal.

In 1888 *Scotsman John Dunlop invented the pneumatic air tire in order to cushion the ride of his son's bicycle.*

The great advantage *of pneumatic tires was that their air cushioning allowed for wheels to be made smaller—spelling the end of the high-wheeler.*

This Humber from the late 19th century has a diamond safety frame, rear suspension, pneumatic tires, and lever-actuated brakes.

By the turn of the 19th century, many of the basic components of the modern bicycle had been introduced, if not perfected. The safety bicycles of the late 1880s and 1890s look remarkably similar to those around today: pneumatic tires, chain drive, tangentially spoked wheels with steel ball-bearing hubs, and the modern diamond frame constructed of hollow tubing, which first appeared on the Humber safety in 1888 and was also used by J. K. Starley's Rover Cob in that same year (J. K. was the nephew of James Starley). The turn of the century marked the end of cycling's Golden Age, and for the next 30 years or so, innovations were small and rarely revolutionary. With the advent of the automobile, the material excesses of the Gilded Age, and the sobering reality of World War I, the bicycle held only a fraction of its former popularity and faded from view until 1930.

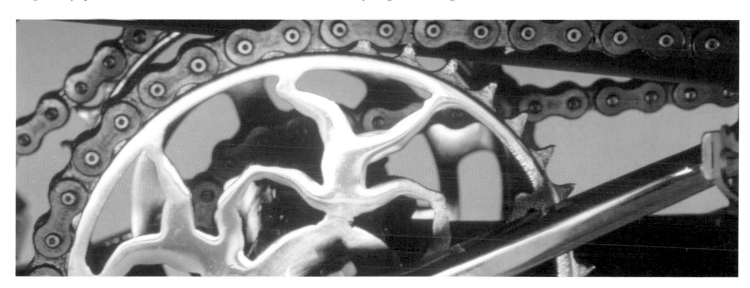

The Best There Ever Was

Put Lance Armstrong, Greg LeMond, Miguel Indurain, and Fausto Coppi in a room, and they will stand in the shadow of a giant who will likely never be surpassed— Eddy Merckx. "The Cannibal," as he was known, for devouring rivals, collected 525 victories, including five Tours de France, during his astonishing 14-year career.

What sets Merckx apart is the sheer scope of his ability. He wasn't just a Tour rider or a Classics man; he won everything—single-day events, stage races, long tours, and hour-long efforts. He competed in 1,800 races and captured a record 34 stages of the Tour de France. From 1969 through 1975, he won 35 percent of his races. During his first Tour de France, he finished 18 minutes ahead and had

Eddy! Eddy! Eddy! Allez Eddy! *Merckx is cheered on by a trio of enthusiastic spectators.*

worn all three jerseys for overall champion, king of the mountain, and points winner. No one could beat Merckx but Merckx.

Eventually, of course, the great Cannibal would lose his teeth. His grueling schedule compounded by lingering injuries from crashes took their toll in 1975, when Merckx was vying for an unprecedented sixth Tour de France victory. He no longer could dominate the mountains or excel in the time trials. He came in second that year to Bernard Thevenet and retired three years later at the age of 32.

Today, Merckx lends his keen building expertise to his namesake line of professional-caliber racing bikes and continues to support elite racers in his homeland of Belgium. His son Axel became Belgian National Champion in 2002.

VITAL STATS

NATIONALITY: Belgian

DATE OF BIRTH: June 17, 1945

CAREER VICTORY HIGHLIGHTS: Tour de France: 1969, 1970, 1971, 1972, 1974

Giro d'Italia: 1968, 1972, 1973, 1974

Milan–San Remo: 1966, 1967, 1969, 1971, 1972, 1975, 1976

Paris–Roubaix: 1968, 1970, 1973

World Hour Record: 1972

THE REVIVAL YEARS

While the invention of the bicycle was the result of contributions from every corner of the Western world, the revival of the bicycle can be traced elegantly to a single, small invention: the balloon tire.

In 1933, when the Great Depression forced many cycle makers to shut their doors, Ignaz Schwinn's eponymous bicycle company introduced a seemingly insignificant 26 by 2.125-inch tire size, called the balloon tire for its fat casing and soft bouncy ride.

This invention was followed by a succession of cruisers, complete with cantilevered frame designs, faux gas tanks, and backswept handlebars. The most notable of these was the 1938 Excelsior, which four decades later would become the chassis for the mountain bike.

Not quite what *Ignaz Schwinn had in mind, but this depression-era dreamer had the right idea.*

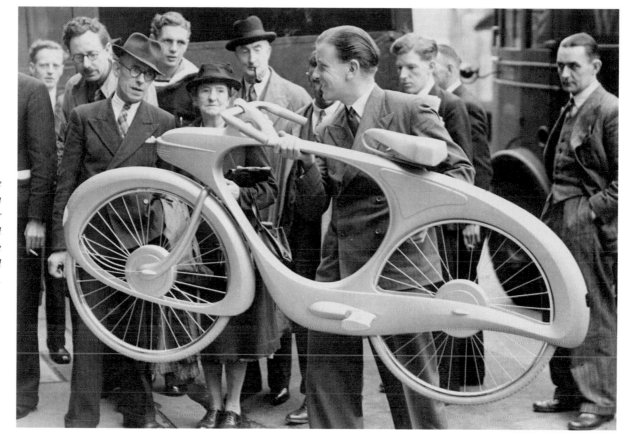

An early *prototype of the Bowden Spacelander. Just over 500 of the original working models were ever produced and fewer than 50 remain.*

Campagnolo's cable-actuated *rear derailleur is a bellwether in the development of the modern racing bike.*

The revival years were marked primarily by design refinements—artistic approaches to the bike that produced beautiful, futuristic oddities like 1946's legendary Bowden Spacelander.

Of the more practical inventions, the most interesting was probably the modern parallelogram derailleur, the Campagnolo Gran Sport, in 1951. The Gran Sport was preceded by a number of crude gear-changing mechanisms, from 1911's Chemineau to the Simplex Tour de France derailleur of the 1930s. Derailleur development was hindered in part by racing, as the Tour de France did not allow derailleurs until 1929, requiring riders to dismount and flip the wheel between the freewheel mounted on each side—the venerable "flip-flop" hub.

Tullio Campagnolo, who essentially invented the modern derailleur, also conceived the quick-release, tools-free wheel skewer after a hellish moment in the 1927 Gran Premio della Vittoria race. The wing nuts on his front wheel froze as he tried to change a tire on a bitterly cold day in the Dolomites. The refinement from the drop parallelogram to the slant parallelogram helped pave the way for modern indexed shifting.

Aside from these few inventions, the revival years were characterized primarily by stylistic improvements that, as we'll see, would prove to be immensely practical.

Campagnolo *on the Croce d'Aune Pass in 1927—a blustery snowy day that bore a historic innovation*

THE MODERN AGE

In the early 1970s, a number of cyclists in the San Francisco area took an interest in old Schwinn balloon-tire cruisers, in particular, the sturdy 1938 Excelsior, which became the test chassis for many of their experiments. The balloon tire's considerable width and volume made it aptly suited for riding off-road.

The earliest protagonists were the Cupertino Riders, a loosely knit band of 10 cyclists who delighted in racing fat-tire cruisers down the fire roads of the surrounding California coast range. On December 1, 1974, three of the group (which also went by the name Morrow Dirt Club, named for the Morrow coaster brake the riders used) showed up at the West Coast Open Cyclocross Championships—a tiny event of a niche sport that would nonetheless be groundbreaking in its

The Cupertino Riders *are said to be the first bunch to tack a rear derailleur onto a fat-tire bike.*

aftermath. The Open Championships were so aptly named because any rider could ride any bike, as opposed to the normal strict categories and rules that determined which bikes were acceptable. Russ Mahon, leader of the Cupertino band, rode a 1930s cruiser brake with derailleurs grafted onto the frame and motorcycle-style drum brakes. Also racing that day (on conventional cyclocross bikes) were Joe Breeze, Charlie Kelly, and Gary Fisher, who were also experimenting with riding cruisers off-road. Mahon, unknowingly, contributed hugely to the nascent collective consciousness of what would become mountain biking: By adding gears, he made it possible to ride up the hills as well as down. Breeze, Kelly, and Fisher were already riding down fire roads in their Marin County home—a pursuit that would soon be immortalized in the first known mountain-

Marin County, *California's Charlie Kelly, an early chronicler of the fat-tire scene*

Gary "Pops" Fisher, *one of mountain biking's greatest proponents and personalities*

Single Day Sensations

World Cup winners are the one-hit wonders of the cycling community. Most don't have the elite physical prowess to dominate a grueling three-week Tour. But on any given race day, they can fight for the line with the best and the brightest. And the one racer who shines the brightest throughout the season gets the big pot of gold—and a rainbow jersey—at the end.

The World Cup road races are a series of 10 single-day events. The series itself is relatively new, first kicking off in 1989 (although it long existed as the Pernod Super Prestige Trophy). Though the individual races are not as long as the great tours, they are equally spectacular and often punishing. Like the grand tours, the World Cup events are exclusively European domain. They include esteemed, century-old classic races such as Liège to Bastogne to Liège, which winds more than 150 miles through rugged Belgian countryside; the grueling, bone-chattering Paris to Roubaix; Italy's magnificent Milan San Remo and Giro di Lombardia; Spain's San Sebastian; and relative newcomer, the Netherlands' hilly and demanding Amstel Gold. Top-finishing racers earn points in each event, and the one who accumulates the highest number is rewarded a white jersey bearing the world champion rainbow stripes.

Mountain bikers, too, have developed a World Cup championship series, consisting of eight events that take more than 150 top-shelf men and women around the globe to various, ever-changing locales, including Hungary, Portugal, Germany, and Great Britain. The World Cup is considered one of the three most prestigious off-road titles, the other two being the NORBA national series and the Olympics.

Recent winners include Belgium's Johan Museeuw, Germany's Erik Zabel, and the United States's Alison Dunlap (off-road).

Leigh Donovan *celebrates her win at the 1996 World Cup Mountain Bike races.*

bike race—the legendary Repack Downhill down Mount Tamalpais in Marin County. Mahon's invention meant that they could ride without pushing their bikes up the hills.

Gary Fisher put Mahon's ideas to work in 1976 on his own bike, and for years he was widely credited with the invention of the mountain bike. Fisher, along with Charlie Kelly and Tom Ritchey, did create the first company devoted to producing mountain bikes and even attempted to patent the term *mountain bike*. But truth be told, the mountain bike, much as the original bicycle itself, was the result of several different isolated inventors, such as Mahon, Fisher, and others, contributing various essential parts of the equation to create something that far surpassed the sum of the pieces.

One seminal creator was Breeze, a frame builder who in 1977 crafted the first real mountain bike, a handmade frame built with all-new components, specifically for the purpose of riding off-road. The Breezer, as his creation was called, had a chrome-moly steel frame, Simplex touring derailleurs, triple crankset, cantilever brakes, and wide knobby tires. Breeze made just 10 bikes for himself and some like-minded friends, but by the time number 10 was done, orders from interested riders began to trickle in. *(continued on page 170)*

Few have done *as much to evolve the bicycle and people's attitudes toward it as has Joe Breeze, seen here with one of his own creations.*

JEANNIE LONGO
An Enduring Pioneer

Though physically a diminutive 5-foot, 2-inch, 102-pound woman, Jeannie Longo is a cyclist of superior strength and indomitable spirit. Taking to the bike during an era when the male-dominated sport frowned on female competitors, Longo smashed through gender barriers and broke records for a remarkable quarter century.

A natural athlete, Longo grew up hiking, swimming, skiing, and cycling. In 1979, she decided to aim for the 1980 World Cycling Championships simply because they were taking place in her hometown. To qualify, she got her license and jumped into the France Championships, which she soundly won at age 21. Supremely confident and street-fighter tough, Longo has a reputation for being a volatile rebel, often battling with teammates, sponsors, and the media. Once she was almost disqualified from World Championships for refusing to wear her sponsor's shoes. But even those who dislike her style cannot argue with her substance.

Longo has racked up an astonishing 710 career wins—more than any other cyclist—male or female—in history. She has 46 National Championship titles and a drawerful of Olympic medals. Her longevity in the sport is equally unprecedented. In 1996, Longo took gold and silver in the Olympic Games in Atlanta and beat the world hour record. She

VITAL STATS

NATIONALITY: French

DATE OF BIRTH: October 31, 1958

CAREER VICTORY HIGHLIGHTS: Tour de France: 1987, 1988, 1989
Olympic Road: 1996
World Champion: 1985, 1986, 1987, 1988, 1989, 1995, 1996, 1997, 2001; World Hour Record: 1995, 1996; French Champion: 1979, 1980, 1981, 1982, 1983, 1984, 1985, 1986, 1987, 1988, 1989, 1992, 1995

also turned 38 years old. Now in her mid-40s, she still does not talk retirement. She credits her longevity in sport to her mental toughness and meticulous organic diet. Love her or hate her, Longo is an icon the sport will not soon forget.

Jeannie Longo *is likely the most winning professional cyclist in history.*

Ritchey was the sport's first prolific builder, crafting hundreds of frames for Fisher and Kelly's Fisher MountainBikes company. The three later went their separate ways, but in 1979 Kelly published an article on the innovative sport in *Outside* magazine and the word was out. In 1982 the first mass-produced mountain bikes, the Specialized Stumpjumper and the Univega Alpina Pro, were unveiled. At $850 and $695, respectively, they were the first widely sold and affordable mountain bikes in existence, and an acquisitive, interested riding public snatched them up.

The resultant boom echoed the original *velocipedomania* with thousands of people worldwide jumping into the newly created sport. In just two short decades, mountain biking went from a sport practiced in isolated spots by a handful of riders who didn't fit into conventional society to one that claimed the lion's share of the multibillion-dollar bicycle industry and a spot in the Olympics—both blessed by and burdened with a sense of legitimacy.

On the mechanical front, the mountain bike injected a sense of innovation and creativity that rivaled that of the Golden Age. Mountain-bike inventors showed a remarkable willingness to crib and *(continued on page 174)*

Motocross anyone?
(right) *This mountain-bike race resembles its gas-powered predecessors.*

The History of Head Protection

Soon after man started spinning atop two wheels, he got a quick lesson in physics—gravity always wins. The knocks got particularly rough at the turn of the 19th century when cities rolled cement over soft, dusty roads. Out of necessity, head protection was invented.

The first helmets were made of pith—a crushable Styrofoam-like material; not exactly ideal, but it softened the blow. Later, racing cyclists donned head coverings made from strips of leather-covered padding. They were a lovely accessory, but hardly protective and rotted from sweat and rain. So, most riders—including top professional racers—continued to go bareheaded, despite the risk.

Remarkably, it wasn't until the 1970s that manufacturers began to take the issue of bike helmet development seriously. The Snell Foundation issued the first bicycle helmet standard in 1970; but ironically only a nonvented, 2-pound motorcycle helmet could pass the test. So concerned cyclists were forced to scour the sporting goods stores for reasonable equivalents, such as goalie helmets.

Finally, in 1975, the Bell Biker, the first bicycling-specific, hard-shelled, EPS (picnic cooler–type) foam-lined helmet, was released—and passed safety standards. Other manufacturers followed Bell's lead and through the years have made advances on the

In April 2003, *the UCI mandated helmets for pro road racers; helmets have always been mandatory for mountain-bike racers at all levels.*

form. The hard outer shell has become lighter, more vents have been added, and adjustable fastening systems now lock helmets securely on the rider's head. Today's helmets are safe, stylish, and comfortable.

Still, many professional cyclists persistently eschew helmet use, even in light of high-profile tragic deaths such as that of Fabio Casartelli in 1995—preferring headbands, caps, or the wind through their hair. That changed in 2003, however, as the International Cycling Union (UCI) has announced that professional cyclists have to wear hard-shell helmets in every race or face a fine—perhaps putting a lid on the issue once and for all.

Slamming *the pavement with a helmet on will protect his head but will not prevent a bad case of road rash.*

steal innovations from a variety of walks of life and from history. Nearly every basic suspension configuration in the first 20 years of the sport owed something to the old yellowing diagrams and texts from the late 1800s and early 1900s.

Designs and materials were liberally borrowed from the motorcycle world (disc brakes), sailing (carbon-fiber construction and monocoques), and the military (exotic materials such as titanium and magnesium). Since gaining legitimacy and popularity in the early 1990s, major new suspension designs have come at the rate of roughly one per year and show few signs of slowing.

Technology is also more rapidly being spread throughout bicycles; disc brakes, virtually unavailable on any bike at any price 10 years ago, are now widespread. The spirit of exploration and innovation that mountain bikes brought to the sport has continued to drive the technological advancement of the machine to the point that the top-level racing bikes of today share much of their inspiration and execution with works-level Formula One cars. Even the everyday bike found in local stores and bike shops shares many of the benefits of that technology. Bicycles today are lighter, more reliable, and more fun to ride than ever before.

Mountain-bike suspension *designs continue to evolve. This bike from Cannondale has two shocks.*

THE MACHINE

The relationship between art and the cycle is
complex. There are many examples of fine art
that use cycles as all or part of their subject
matter, including a rich variety of commercial art
that advertises and promotes cycling, as well as
illustrative art produced for magazines and books.

Furthermore, cycles have inspired decorative arts and products,
while for many enthusiasts and design pundits, cycles themselves
count as art objects. Of course, it all depends on what your
definition of *art* is. The cycle builder's art is very different from the
fine art produced by artists Marcel Duchamp and Pablo Picasso,
both of whom incorporated references to cycles in their work.

Usable art *that can be afforded by most people in the world*

CHAPTER 4

THE ART
OF THE
CYCLE

By Nicholas Oddy

Machine art *like the bicycle doesn't get made in a typical studio.*

The cycle, particularly the bicycle, has appealed to many design critics as an example of a "machine aesthetic" in which beauty is the natural outcome of an uncompromised and undecorated mechanical form. In fact, the cycle, like all man-made objects, is subject to human tastes and fashions, but its *seeming* simplicity disguises this. Those who think of the machine itself as a work of art usually think in the traditional manner that art means skill as well as beauty. They tend not only to look at the machine as a whole but also to derive much satisfaction from details that point to the skill of the maker and the quality of material, such as the lugwork, the expert welding, the crisply formed components, and the little idiosyncratic touches that separate the first division from the rest. Extra pleasure comes from knowledge and experience, which separate the connoisseur from the novice or the philistine who thinks that all bicycles are much the same.

Framers *transform metal with precision to create machine artwork.*

THE BUILDERS
AND THEIR WARES

The modern cycle has its roots in the 1817 bicycle design of Karl von Drais. Von Drais's running machine, called the Draisienne, had some attention paid to its looks, even in its earliest form—von Drais recommended that machines be painted in patriotic national colors. However, credit should probably go to Denis Johnson of London for giving careful consideration to both the practicality and beauty of the machine, which has become a hallmark of the cycle builder ever since. Johnson's machines, known as hobbyhorses, enjoyed a brief but significant vogue in 1819. They used more metal components than von Drais's and were carefully shaped in sweeping curves, which allowed the machines to take on a lighter and more elegant appearance while also looking quick. The builder's ability to make the machine look light and fast, even when stationary, is essential to the art of cycle design. Johnson's machines and their riders also inspired and encouraged much interest from illustrators.

Two periods of cycle production stand out as providing the most aesthetically pleasing and satisfying examples of the art—these were on either side of the high-wheeled machine created in the 1870s and early 1880s. Both were notable in that the machines of those times were notoriously unsatisfying to ride, particularly the one that came later, but were hard to beat for sheer elegance and proportion. This raises the specter of taste. Many believe the high-wheeler itself is in a class of its own, while many others consider the European lightweight cycle of the 1950s to be the pinnacle of beauty. For some, today's state-of-

With its simple lines, *a Draisienne (above) was as much craft as early-19th-century cutting-edge technology.*

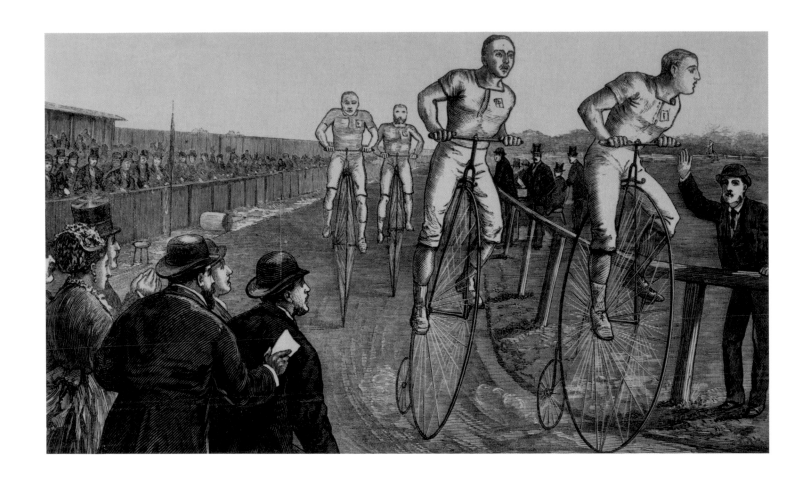

High-wheelers *were aesthetic triumphs but something of mechanical menaces.*

the-art track machines rise to the top. All have their merits, but I suppose that I like the velocipede of the mid 1860s and the hard-tired safety of the late 1880s because of their aesthetic triumphs over their deficiencies.

Both types of machine were very heavy and unresponsive to ride. While this is excusable in the case of the velocipede, which was made at a time when it was the only design available, it is less so in the case of the hard-tired safety, which was produced simultaneously with the high-wheeler. Comparing the three, the high-wheeler is a design form that, because of the fineness of

the driving wheel and its dominance over the rest of the machine, is difficult to mess up. (Even a dog of a high-wheeler looks good at a few paces.) High-wheelers are differentiated only by their craftsmanship and minor details. Whereas most all-metal machines were plain black, the wooden-wheeled velocipede was more subject to the aesthetic manipulation of its components, which tended toward the carriage-building practices of bright paint and bold lining.

But for sheer variation, where the best is truly magnificent and the worst truly execrable, the hard-tired safety, in both

bicycle and tricycle form, is a study in what makes a beautiful machine. The combination of hard tires and clumsy chains of the early safeties did their riders no favors. However, the safeties could be geared up to go faster than a high-wheeler, even if an exceedingly disproportionate amount of energy was used in doing so. Most riders were attracted by this potential speed, while a growing number of new riders were attracted by the lack of distance to the ground. To illustrate how important the look of the safety was to its market, we need only consider the pioneering designs of Harry John Lawson in the 1870s, which were dismissed for their crocodile-like appearance rather than their technical potential. It required the marketing skills of John Kemp Starley to sell the concept of the chain-driven safety as a potentially faster machine than the high-wheeler. Once this had been accepted, designs for chain-driven safeties proliferated. The combination of thin tubing and large diameter slender rims with narrow hard tires is particularly pleasing.

Possibly because of the rough ride that one could expect from a low machine with no suspension, manufacturers were keen to experiment with curved tubes and long, sweeping handlebars that looked elegant and racy and absorbed vibration. Manipulating the components to look good rather than to perform any better became a particular art.

French arms manufacturer Manufrance *created this curvaceous beauty l'Hirondelle.*

More Mystery than the Mona Lisa

Renaissance man Leonardo da Vinci is remembered as an oil-paint genius whose strokes of brilliance include the Mona Lisa and *The Last Supper*. What is largely forgotten is that this accomplished artist was also one of the greatest scientific minds of all time. During an era when the only choices for transportation were feet or pack animals, da Vinci created sketches of an airplane, a helicopter, a parachute, and some believe, a bicycle.

Though father and son Parisian carriage makers Pierre and Ernest Michaux are typically credited with developing the modern bicycle in the 1860s, monks found in 1966 a rough draft of a chain-driven, pedal-powered, two-wheeled machine among da Vinci's writings for the government. Historians date the sketch back to the 1490s—about 370 years before the first velocipede rolled out.

Today, questions abound as to whether the bike drawing is da Vinci's brainchild, a student's creation, or a Sasquatch-sized hoax. The line drawing was discovered among other cartoonlike doodles filling the margin of da Vinci's *Codex Atlanticus*, a collection of sketches of weapons, warfare, and other

devices. The name *Salai,* one of Leonardo's prized pupils, was penned on the back of the page. Some historians speculate that Salai had just copied the two-wheeled wonder from one of his master's many now-lost designs. Skeptics, however, suggest the drawing is nothing but a fake—a modern-day hoax designed to further elevate popular perception of da Vinci's genius.

Since most of his work went unpublished, the world will likely never unravel the mystery of da Vinci's sketch. But based on the vast collection of inventive scientific musings he left behind, one thing is clear: A bicycle was certainly not beyond the realm of his imagination.

Did da Vinci *or one of his students sketch the first two-wheeler?*

A significant development of the hard-tired period was the introduction of open-framed ladies' machines. These lent themselves to elegant and curvy forms well illustrated by the French l'Hirondelle bicycle. Best of all in this period were the tricycles by the great makers such as Singer. Magnificent in proportion, detail, and layout, they were wonderful objects to look at but hell to ride any distance!

Open-framed machines continued to challenge the cycle builder, given that they were inherently weak and given to "whip." Attempts to correct this have often produced artful results, not least of which is the so-called *mixte* lightweight frame of the 1930s, which is still made today. Even the classic semicurved, or "loop," format, typical of ladies' roadsters from the 1890s through the 1950s and still common in the Netherlands, makes a cheaply made machine into a worthwhile object.

Hard-tired safeties were state-of-the-art adult machines for their time, but for the art of dressing up a machine, the peculiarly American phenomenon of the balloon-tired bicycle was unrivaled. This bicycle was aimed at young people aspiring to travel quickly. The American motorcycle-like bicycle had been developing for two decades before the

An incredible example *of streamlining, the Schwinn Aerocycle was created for the 1933–34 World's Fair.*

Schwinn Aerocycle was launched in 1933. Typical of other heavily styled goods produced in the Depression, it was probably more than a coincidence that the concept of stylistic obsolescence was considered a tool for economic recovery. The success of the Schwinn inspired others to follow suit for a generation. Like the hard-tired safety, the results are impressive. Today, balloon-tired bikes are collected as decorative art objects. In Europe, many see balloon-tired bikes as an offense against cycle design because the aesthetic so obviously dominates the design at the expense of efficiency.

Cycle connoisseurs who value efficiency are often drawn to the European-style lightweight cycle; ironically, the classic period of its production exactly parallels that of the balloon-tired bike. Even though they are often more than half a century old, these

While not necessarily *expensive, European lightweight bicycles have a time-worn elegance.*

machines, built on slender racing rims with multiple-speed derailleur gears and dropped racing bars, still look quite modern. Although some were built in large factories, most were the products of small frame-building workshops, often under the control of a builder-owner whose surname became that of the machine. This more closely aligns the lightweight-bicycle collector with the fine art collector, in that the machines are products of named individuals. Experts can spot a particular builder's technique, or "hand," in a frame the same way that decorative and fine art connoisseurs can in artwork. This lightweight "tradition" continues to this day, as individual builders continue to produce custom-made frames in small numbers. The skill, workmanship, and elegance of the resulting product continue to represent the best of the cycle builder's art.

DEPICTIONS OF CYCLING

When Denis Johnson presented his improved design of the Draisienne to the London market in 1819, it gained immediate attention not only from the fashionable young men who became associated with it (hence the nickname dandy horse), but also from commentators more interested in its comic potential. The result was the production of a remarkable amount of hobbyhorse-related artifacts and artwork.

Of these, the most significant by far are the prints made by publishers such as Thomas Tegg. Roger Street, in his seminal study of the British hobbyhorse, lists almost 100 prints—most of them satirical and most all published in 1819. These prints were used to provide images for makers of trinkets and accessories, some of which remained popular well after the hobbyhorse had gone out of fashion. Hobbyhorse images appeared commonly on earthenware ceramics and small personal goods such as snuff and patch boxes.

Playing up *their comic potential, British publisher Thomas Tegg published extensive studies of the hobbyhorse and its practitioners.*

Cycling Memorabilia

As with anything from the finest works of art to the lowly Pez dispenser, the bicycle has its own incredibly colorful subculture of collectors. Bike collectors are not different from other types of collectors in that collecting is often a course that chooses them, not the other way around. "I came across a bicycle that I liked but knew nothing about, and I simply bought it. It went on from there, and like most people, I searched to find something that was like it or associated with it and ended up with a collection," said Pryor Dodge, a New York–based musician and author who specializes in collecting bikes and artwork from the 19th century.

Satisfaction in collecting comes in many forms: Some simply shoot for the biggest, broadest collection while others, like Bradley Woehl, owner of San Francisco's American Cyclery, find that it's the chase for a rare bike or component that's exciting. "I like the whole process of collecting. The hunting down and figuring out of things. The digging through barns or basements to find a bike with a great history. A lot of people acquire bikes for nostalgic reasons or for the sake of vanity, but I chose to make a career out of finding bikes with stories to tell, restoring them, and passing them on. So, I guess I'm more of a custodian than a collector."

These days collectors like Dodge and Woehl tend to break down the object of their desire into a few common categories: extremely rare bikes from the turn of the century and before; pre-war bikes; balloon-tire bikes, such as the Schwinn Phantom; vintage lightweight racing and touring bikes; and a special category just for the muscle bikes of the 1960s and 1970s, such as the Schwinn Sting-Ray and its army of imitators. Wrapped in the sentimentality of a more innocent time, balloon-tire bikes have generally sold for the highest prices, but as the turmoil of the late 1960s and early 1970s fades into memory, the Sting-Ray and European racing bikes of that generation are emerging as favorites of a younger generation of collectors.

Bicycles and related *ephemera are becoming increasingly collectible.*

Decorative items
*like this lamp with
a bicycle design were
all the rage during
the early days
of the bicycle.*

Through the 19th century, this pattern repeated with every cycling craze, but the amount of satirical material diminished in proportion to that which celebrated cycles and cycling. The fact that cycling was largely a pastime of the wealthy throughout the century doubtless encouraged many makers to try to tap the purses of its followers. It is not unusual to find quite elaborate porcelain figures, marble timepieces, gold and silver jewelry, and so on, designed around a cycling theme. Such items were particularly prolific during the bicycle boom of the mid-1890s, by which time there was a substantial and rapidly increasing number of female cyclists. Curiously, though, most of this type of decorative design was quite conservative in its style, favoring the rococo and the neoclassical in spite of the obvious modernity of its subject matter.

THE COMMERCIAL ARTISTS

High-quality, cycling-inspired decorative goods lasted longest in France and Germany where art nouveau, secessionist, and even early art deco–style work was produced. However, once the cycle was relegated to being a child's plaything in America and a poor man's transport in Europe during the interwar years, high quality ended in all but trophy design. Typical products of the mid to late 20th century were generally nostalgic and conservative in design and third rate in quality, being aimed at the low end of the gift and souvenir market.

If decorative design was cautious, the opposite was true of commercial art used to sell cycles to the "boom" market of the 1890s. The cycle industry was truly on the cutting edge of the discipline, only equaled by theater and concert advertising—way ahead of areas that were to excel in the 20th century, such as railway and shipping lines. The cycle industry equated its products with high fashion and modernity and thus led the way in art catalog and color-litho poster design. American makers probably were ahead in using leading-edge graphics, particularly in catalog design. The major American makers were aggressive in the international market and more conscious of the value of high-quality advertising than most others. Major marques such as Crescent, Waverley, and Victor employed the most noted commercial artists of the time, such as Will Bradley. American catalogs and advertising done in art nouveau, French revue, Japanese, and aesthetic styles were commonplace but were carried out with a panache that made them largely acceptable to American and European society.

Early-20th-century *cycle advertising was as cutting edge as the most adventurous graphic design of the era.*

The Art Nouveau period *(1895–1910)*
produced some of the most elegant and
imaginative images of the bicycle ever captured.

For sheer innovation and outrageous imagery, though, American cycle advertising paled in comparison to the French litho posters of the period. In French cycling ads, naked or almost naked female figures were not unusual; symbolism, often of a blatant and morally suspect kind, abounded. The famous poster for Gladiator is probably the best known of these, but the extraordinary offering for Catenol, titled *La Verite Assise*, is perhaps the most challenging! Furthermore, some manufacturers even commissioned bohemian fine artists to produce posters, the most famous being Henri de Toulouse-Lautrec for the French agency of the British Simpson Chain Syndicate.

Henri Toulouse-Lautrec *produced some of the best-known bicycle related advertising like this much-reproduced work for British Simpson Chain Syndicate.*

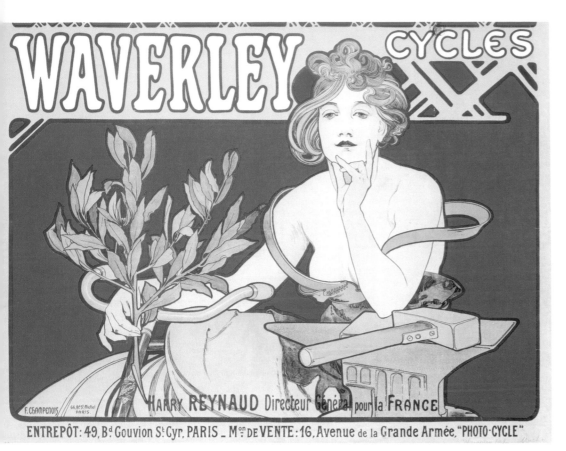

Indeed, it is worth noting that numerous non-French makers other than Simpson commissioned special French posters through their French agencies; it is this practice that resulted in the well-known poster for Waverley by Alphonse Mucha. Not surprisingly, the more dynamic French posters were not commonly seen outside of Paris and other French metropolitan centers. However, on an international level, critics saw them as significant, even at the time of their currency, and they remain the most desirable cycle art to this day, appealing to a very broad and wealthy audience.

Mucha's incredible *Nouveau poster for Waverley is a high-water mark for early cycle advertising.*

POPULAR CULTURE
Our Common Thread

Though relatively few people ride bicycles daily, the two-wheeled companion leaves invisible tracks connecting nearly every man, woman, and child. Almost everyone learns how to ride a bike, and most people vividly remember their first two-wheeler. Part of our common bond, bicycles permeate our popular culture. Look around. You'll spy shiny triangular frames in our art, our entertainment, and our literature.

Childhood books, in particular, are brimming with bicycles. Colorful, mischievous characters like Curious George, created more than 60 years ago by Hans and Margret Rey (who themselves fled Nazi Germany via bicycles), carry out their devilish deeds atop two wheels. Classic American storytellers like Mark Twain wrote entire essays on their bicycle follies. Sometimes, even the bike alone was enough to be

entertaining, as was the case with the notorious, never ridden but much talked about Klein mountain bike that hung in Jerry Seinfeld's apartment for most of the hit sitcom's nine-year run.

With their playful colors, shiny gears, and simple architecture, bicycles have caught the eye of many an artist, as well. Since their invention, bicycles have appeared in many famous paintings, and in the case of works like *Bicycle Riders* by Gyorgy Lehoczky and *Bicycle Made for Two* by Paul Greenwood, they have been the starring subject on many a canvas. Perhaps the most famous, and certainly the most simple, artistic rendition of a bicycle was the whimsical bike rider created by pop artist Keith Haring. His image of a person crouched down on two wheels is evocative of how devoted cyclists feel about their bikes—joyfully part of the machine.

As we move into the 21st century, the bicycle rolls along with us, appearing in commercials, movies, and modern art as a reminder of one thing we all have in common.

It's no mistake *that the ever-mischievous Curious George is often seen riding a bicycle.*

THE ILLUSTRATORS

Less dramatic but equally skilled are the illustrations produced largely for the cycle press. Cycling was probably the first modern sport to develop a specialized press with a broad range of magazines and newspapers devoted wholly to it. During the 1880s, this became well established enough for some titles to commission regular illustrators whose line drawings have become the benchmark of cycling depiction. The English illustrator George Moore was probably the first to become a "name," and in much the same style, the Anglo-American Joseph Pennell's work is well known through the books written by him and his wife, Elizabeth, on their various tricycling and bicycling adventures in the 1880s and 1890s. In the first half of the 20th century, Frank Patterson's drawings for the British weekly *Cycling* have come to evoke all the aspirations of cycling at the time. Much of his work survives today and is still affordable by those who want to own an original piece of art by one of the great names of cyclo-illustration. Cyclo-illustration continues, but with the advances made in photography and color printing, it is unlikely that another illustrator like Patterson or Moore will emerge.

Joseph Pennell (left) *at work on a drawing in his atelier. Pennell's work* (opposite page) *portrays a parade of high-wheelers passing by a raucous crowd.*

FINE ART AND CYCLES

Probably the first time that cycles became a subject of fine art was during the period of the velocipedes in the second half of the 1860s. The most famous work of this period is the portrait of Blanche d'Antigny, a well-known and wealthy French courtesan, posed aside a Michaux-type machine wearing divided garments.

Women *posing with bikes*

Clearly this portrait uses the cycle and the riding costume as a statement of the sitter's modernity, fashionability, independence, and daring. Surprisingly though, portraiture of any kind was rare, even in the 1890s, when large numbers of wealthy women took to cycling. Few women chose to have themselves painted with their machines.

Perhaps this was because cycling portraiture was almost entirely the preserve of the new art of photography. The modernity of both was seen as

complementary, and today late 19th-century professional photo portraits of riders with their machines are still easily found. An illustration of the primacy of photography is the 1893 oil painting of the professional racer F. J. Osmond riding along a country road on his Whitworth bicycle. This illustration was directly painted from studio photographs with the mythical landscape the only original contribution by the artist.

Invented and perfected *along the same time lines, the bicycle and the camera have had a stunning partnership.*

More typical of this period are paintings depicting general cycling scenes such as fashionable riders promenading in parks—for instance, Jean Beraud's *Le Chalet du Cycle au Bois de Boulogne* and amusing genre paintings, such as J. Wely's *Collecting Plums*. One of the most reproduced is the very quick and effective 1899 watercolor sketch by the Scottish artist J. Waterston Herald, of a girl riding her bicycle while her dog scampers along her side, which can be seen today in the Burrell Collection, Glasgow, Scotland. Something of the same freedom is present in the earlier *Lady on a Safety Tricycle*, by James Lavery, in 1885. Beyond his role as commercial artist for the British Simpson Chain Syndicate, Toulouse-Lautrec produced a body of work depicting track cycling, its promoters, and its participants. Quite apart from the important commercial considerations, Toulouse-Lautrec's interest was fired by the modernity, popularity, and decadence of cycle racing at this period, where doping was freely indulged and corruption was rife. Many events were seen as almost as morally bankrupt as Toulouse-Lautrec's other interest, revue bars.

Beraud's painting *of cyclists in Paris' Bois de Boulogne, still a popular riding spot for Parisians*

LANCE ARMSTRONG
Art in Motion

No book on cycling would be complete without Lance Armstrong. Armstrong has claimed his fifth Tour de France victory and many predict the hellion from Texas will roll on to an unprecedented sixth. But his dominance in the hardest race on earth is merely a sidebar to his most amazing feat—a comeback from cancer.

Armstrong had all the makings of a rising star. The Golden Boy from America was a professional triathlete by age 16 and just six years later was a pro cyclist, holding 10 titles, including the U.S. Pro Championship, World Champion (the youngest ever), and a stage victory at the Tour de France. He continued winning races and was named American Male Cyclist of the Year by *VeloNews* in 1995.

The next year his life would change forever. Forced from the bike by excruciating pain, Armstrong learned that he had advanced testicular cancer that had spread to his lungs and brain. His chances to live, let alone ride, were slim. But the tenacious Texan endured aggressive treatment including surgeries and intensive chemotherapy. Though physically depleted, his mental reserves swelled. The cancer went into remission, and the raging competitor emerged.

Armstrong returned to the 1999 Tour de France and shocked the world with a no-holds-barred victory, followed by four more in the successive years.

Though his story is still being written, he will be an inspiration for the ages. Armstrong supports the cancer community through the Lance Armstrong Foundation for research and education.

VITAL STATS

NATIONALITY: American

DATE OF BIRTH: September 18, 1971

CAREER VICTORY HIGHLIGHTS: Tour de France: 1999, 2000, 2001, 2002, 2003; Midi Libre: 2002; Dauphiné. 2002; Tour of Switzerland: 2001; Tour du Pont: 1995, 1996; World Road Champion: 1993

AS ART TODAY

Over the last century, the use of cycles in fine art has moved away from the straight depictions of the 1890s toward a more conceptual role. In the early 20th century, it was still enough of a dynamic machine to be the subject of Italian Futurism, a movement that celebrated the mechanization of society.

More recently, the linking of human energy, vulnerability, and balance that the bicycle represents creates a valuable symbolism that has been exploited by artists as diverse as Fernand Léger and Francis Bacon. Equally it was one of the first objects to be used as readymades in sculpture. Here the artist usually plays on the prosaic and commonplace nature of the object to force the viewer to reassess and question its meaning.

Cubist Léger (right) *often depicted modern urban, technological culture.*
American Robert Rauschenberg's *pop art* (left) *is known for mixed media and has featured bicycles.*

By 1913, the bicycle was universal enough for Marcel Duchamp to employ a set of upturned front forks and wheel in the same way as he did a urinal four years later—although the title *Bicycle Wheel* is less of an overt challenge than *Fountain*. Picasso, on the other hand, exploited the anthropomorphic nature of cycle components, taking cow-horn bars as literally that.

Clearly, the cycle will continue to be a part of the fine artist's repertoire, but that is really all that it is—a prop that can be utilized where appropriate. This makes its use in fine art very different from cyclo-illustration, where the cycle is the central theme of the work. It is not a surprise that cycle enthusiasts tend to take more notice of the latter as a result.

CHAPTER 5

MOUNTAIN BIKES

By Zapata Espinoza

WHEN IT ALL BEGAN

The story of mountain biking is full of events, places, and personalities. Its history—decades old—was innocent, pure, and without bias. By the mid-1970s, when it began anew, it was innocent no more.

The question of when mountain biking was born remains one of the great two-wheel mysteries. For all we know, it could have been in the middle of a Tour de France back in the 1920s when the first Italian to win the acclaimed race, Ottavia Bottecchia, and his hard-man cohorts were pedaling along dirt roads up the Alps, suffering in a manner not unlike today's Trans-Alp mountain-bike racers.

Maybe it was on the outskirts of Paris in the 1950s when members of the Velo Cross Club Parisien mounted primitive suspension parts on their bikes and gathered for weekend forays on the quieted hare scrambles courses after their motorcycling brethren had gone home for the day. These were the forbears of the mountain-cross racers we now watch on the Outdoor Life Network.

The Velo Cross Club *of Paris may have been the* first *mountain-bike club. They definitely had the outsider spirit associated with fat-tire pioneers.*

The answer remains elusive, but one thing is clear: In the beginning, it was a simple matter of dirt roads and a need to get somewhere, with no other way to get there but through the bush and along some trail. If we dismiss the need for dates, we can simply trace the roots of the sport in these terms: Cycling off-road for work became fun, and technology evolved to make it fast and with purpose. That is really when the sport of mountain biking was born. Although the trails are important, focusing on them alone would be tantamount to conversing about goat herding. No! To talk about mountain biking with reason is to acknowledge the arrival of sport-specific technology. Gears, tires, frame designs, and suspension are the true markers of the sport's progress.

From the Velo Cross Club *to world champion John Tomac, mountain biking has always been about speed and adrenaline.*

MOUNTAIN BIKES 217

FROM MARIN TO THE BUTTE

True, the San Francisco suburb of Marin County is widely credited as the birthplace of modern mountain biking. However, the original "tilters" in Crested Butte, Colorado, probably still laugh at the thought. Sure, while the Marin hippies were bolting derailleurs onto their 1940 Klunker bikes to have downhill races on Mt. Tam, the Butte hippies were taking their bikes up and over the treacherous 12,700-foot elevation of Pearl Pass and into Aspen.

As Crested Butte local Don Cook says, "The Marin guys were experimenting with technology, but it wasn't until they got here that the technology was introduced to the kind of terrain that would define the sport." *(continued on page 222)*

Before *it was a haven for dot-com millionaires, Marin County was home to mountain biking's pioneers.*

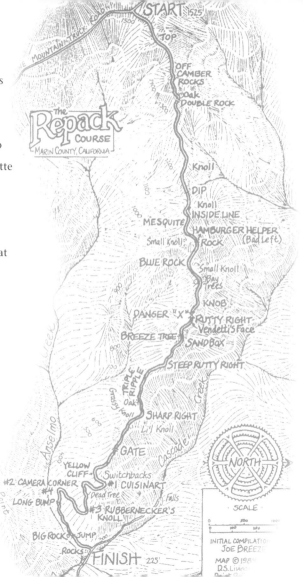

A Century in the Making

Off-road enthusiasts typically credit Marin County, California, bike gurus Gary Fisher, Tom Ritchey, and Joe Breeze as the "fathers of mountain biking." True, this ingenious trio developed the first bikes that were built, sold, and marketed specifically for trail riding. But dirt-loving cyclists had been tooling together fat tires and beefy bikes for at least 100 years before anyone knew those three names.

Some say Scottish veterinarian John B. Dunlop invented the first "mountain bike" in 1887, when he fitted an inflatable piece of rubber hose over the solid tires on his son's bicycle. The air cushion provided much-needed suspension for the predominantly dirt paths of the time. A few years later, in 1896, an infantry division of the Buffalo Soldiers, assigned to patrol some of the national parks, created the first mountain-bike "club," when they rode from Missoula, Montana, to Yellowstone and back—800 monumental miles—to test if the military could traverse challenging terrain atop two wheels. And by the early 1950s, there was off-road racing in Paris, as the Velo Cross Club Parisien juiced up their bikes and tested their mettle on a course that was remarkably similar to a modern mountain-bike circuit.

In America, the first mountain bike was likely developed by John Finley Scott in 1953. He added flat handlebars, balloon tires, and cantilever brakes to a Schwinn World diamond frame and christened it the "Woodsie Bike." He remained alone in his pursuit until the early '70s, when a band of dirt lovers, called the Cupertino Riders, cruised through Southern California on beefy race bikes built by Russ Mahon. That's where Fisher, Ritchey, and Breeze got the idea and ran with it, starting a mountain-bike fever that would spread worldwide in the early 1980s, when bike manufacturers Specialized and Univega unveiled two Japanese-built bicycles for less than $1,000. The rest, as they say, is history.

Object of the first *mountain biking road trip: Pearl Pass above Crested Butte, Colorado*

"The mountain bike didn't just create a new bicycle, it humanized cycling"

JOE BREEZE

Both experiences speak to the day and age when passionate off-road cyclists started tinkering with their bikes. The cycling world was about to enter a new phase that would forever alter its popularity. And when Joe Breeze welded together the first mountain-bike frame in 1977, its unique qualities set the frenzy for specific mountain-bike equipment in motion. There would be no turning back.

Lucky for us, the Marin mountain bikers were all road geeks before they tasted off-road pleasure. The likes of pioneers Gary Fisher, Charlie Kelly, Tom Ritchey, and Breeze could never leave well enough alone. The bikes they rode seldom used the same setup from week to week due to their constant tinkering and parts swapping. By the end of the 1970s, all of Marin was abuzz with the off-road sensation. The news of the mountain-bike creation could no longer be confined to the small brigade that had nurtured it for the previous six years.

From Repack *through the latest 24-hour race, founding father Gary Fisher still practices what he preaches.*

Don Cook keeps the flame at the Mountain Bike Hall of Fame in Crested Butte, Colorado.

With access to trails *and remote places never before possible, mountain biking took off like wildfire.*

ENTER THE ENTREPENEURS

The year was 1982. BANG! It had begun. Cycling entrepreneur Mike Sinyard took the mountain-bike frame he'd bought from Tom Ritchey and sent it to Japan to have some cheap copies made. Granted, Mert Lawwill had made his Pro Cruiser five years earlier, while Univega was playing with dirt bikes, and Schwinn had already been marketing their Sidewinder mountain bike as early as 1981.

But Sinyard's Specialized Stumpjumper was the bike that got the mass-production ball rolling. By the mid-'80s every known bike maker had jumped on the mountain-bike bandwagon. Unfortunately, with no precedent to draw upon, very few of them had any idea exactly what they were doing.

Specialized *bicycles founder Mike Sinyard epitomizes the entrepreneurial spirit that helped grow the sport and the business of mountain biking.*

Beginning *in 1981,*
Specialized's
Stumpjumper brought
the mountain bike to
the masses.

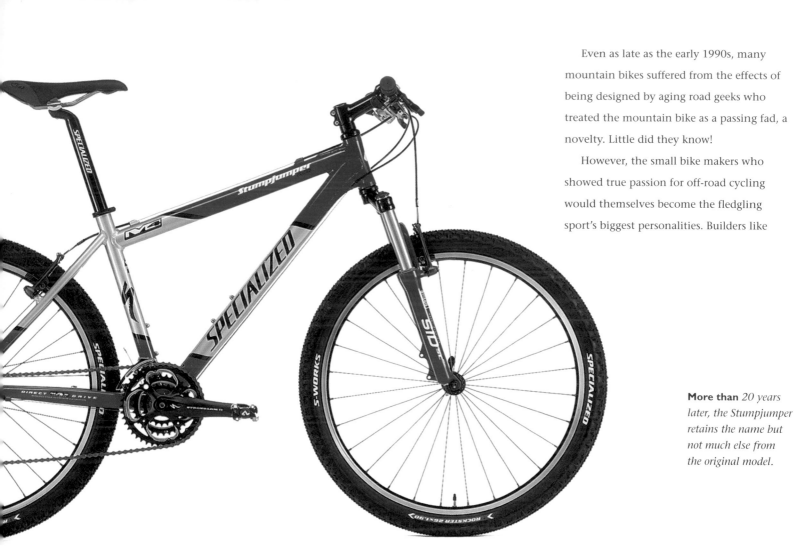

Even as late as the early 1990s, many mountain bikes suffered from the effects of being designed by aging road geeks who treated the mountain bike as a passing fad, a novelty. Little did they know!

However, the small bike makers who showed true passion for off-road cycling would themselves become the fledgling sport's biggest personalities. Builders like

More than *20 years later, the Stumpjumper retains the name but not much else from the original model.*

Chris Chance, Charlie Cunningham, Doug Bradbury, Richard Cunningham, Keith Bontrager, and of course, Gary Fisher and Tom Ritchey helped fuel the sport's soon-to-be explosive growth with wonderfully designed, sport-specific bikes. These were some of the key players who planted the early seeds of what would become a multimillion-dollar cottage industry.

The small guys (clockwise from right) *like Doug Bradbury, Keith Bontrager, Chris Chance, Charlie Cunningham, and Richard Cunningham put the soul in mountain biking.*

SUSPENSION:
THE BIGGEST STEP OF ALL

In 1989, seven years after the Stumpjumper's arrival at the Long Beach bike show, a radical, unimaginable new bike was wheeled into the same convention hall—and the sport would never be the same.

While most manufacturers were still trying to figure out what the ingredients were for even the most basic off-road bicycle, the guys from Kestrel rolled their fully suspended, carbon-fiber Nitro into their booth. Jaws dropped, heads shook, and cameras clicked. It wasn't supposed to happen, at least not this soon.

Although the bike as a whole took top honors for the most innovative bike at the show, it was the RockShox suspension fork mounted up front that would prove to have the most enduring impact.

RockShox: Who would have guessed that what began in a cramped Santa Cruz garage would some day become a multinational company traded on the New York Stock Exchange? *(continued on page 232)*

Paul Turner *bought motorcycle-inspired front suspension to the mountain bike.*

JOHN TOMAC
A Wonder on Wheels

Imagine high-speed hurdler Edwin Moses running off after his Olympic gold medal wins and crushing the field at the Boston marathon. That's the kind of bike rider John Tomac was—a legend who blasted through boundaries between cycling niches and forever changed the face of mountain-bike racing.

Emerging from the BMX scene, where he won his first national title in 1984 at age 16, "Johnny T" has topped the podium at more mountain-bike races than anyone in dirt racing history. For a stretch, it seemed he could ride any bike faster than anyone at any venue. During a time when XC racers were health-conscious featherweights and downhillers were heavily muscled party boys, Tomac grabbed top honors in both disciplines, winning the national XC title in 1996 and the downhill title in 1997.

Early in his career, he even hopped aboard skinny tires, splitting his time between professional road and mountain-bike racing. Again, he was an instant success, capturing the Best Young Rider title at the Coors Classic Prologue in 1988. *VeloNews* crowned him the world's top all-around rider that same year.

Ever the rugged, and often eccentric, individualist, Tomac was willing to race equipment most image-conscious racers wouldn't be caught leaving their driveway on. Some experiments, like drop road-racing bars on his mountain bike, never caught on. But others, most notably using a full-suspension rig to crush his competitors at the downhill World Cup in 1993, changed racers' approach to speed and technology forever.

VITAL STATS

NATIONALITY: American

DATE OF BIRTH: November 3, 1967

CAREER VICTORY HIGHLIGHTS: U.S. Road Championships: 1988; World Mountain-Bike Championships: 1988, 1990; National XC Championships: 1996; National DH Championships: 1997; National BMX Cruiser Championship: 1984

Johnny T: *The most diverse and inspired mountain-bike racer ever*

The impact of suspension on the bicycle industry in the late 1980s would, as a whole, be bigger than that of any other single product. It was the suspension segment that also opened the floodgates for the throttle twisters to come rushing in. Virtually every motorcycle fan came to mountain biking with a shared experience: They'd ridden a bicycle offroad and found it to be not only uncomfortable, but unsafe as well. They knew there had to be a better way, and with their wealth of knowledge and firsthand experience in the dynamics of driving two wheels over rough ground, the motorcycle guys trumped the traditionally minded cyclists on the sport's biggest advancement.

If left to the bike geeks themselves, suspension probably would never have happened. The less visionary felt that suspension was little more than a comfort factor that could not add to the efficiency of cycling; however, the motorcycle guys proved more than able to dispel that half-baked theory. Sure, it was one thing for downhillers to use suspension, the pedal set figured, but really, where else?

Even the most *weight-conscious cross-country rider* (left) *can appreciate the comfort and safety of a suspension fork.*
Proud papa Gary Fisher (right) *hoists two-time Olympic champion Paola Pezzo's full-suspension cross-country race bike.*

In 1993, when wily Frenchman Gilbert Duclos-Lassalle outsprinted Italian Franco Ballerini to win the infamous Paris-to-Roubaix road race on his Lemond road bike, one outfitted with special RockShox suspension forks, it looked as though mountain-bike suspension would even conquer the tradition-bound world of European road racing. However, after a few years of wild experimentation (where a number of front and full suspension designs were tried), road-bike suspension faded into the background. Since Duclos-Lassalle's '93 victory, there have been no major wins on road bicycles outfitted with suspension. Due to the emphasis on minimal weight and maximum efficiency, it's unlikely that suspension will become the norm for road racing any time soon.

By the year 2000, it was all about suspension. The sport of downhilling had morphed into something called *freeriding* and even elite cross-country riders were relying more and more on the performance benefits found with new, niche-specific suspension technology. Where the big air huckers were using coil-sprung, wet-bath suspension parts to get up to 10 inches of super plush front and rear travel, the XC set were coming to terms with shorter travel air shocks with remote lockout and intricate valving that provided a stable pedaling platform not foreseen even a few years earlier.

Duclos-Lassalle *riding to victory in 1993 Paris-to-Roubaix*

Tradition-bound *road racers like American George Hincapie are reluctant to use suspension for even the most difficult races.*

Woodstock on Wheels

Inside every mountain biker is a secret Walter Mitty—a fearless alter ego who can climb like a mountain goat, flow downhill like water, and jump like Evel Knievel. In 1992, race director Laird Knight created a place for all those inner heroes to come out and play. It was 13 miles of slippery rocks and roots, tire-sucking mud, lung-searing climbs, and treacherous descents. Adding darkness and sleep deprivation to the challenge, two- to five-person teams would race relay style for 24 hours, trying to stack up the most laps. He called it the 24 Hours of Canaan, after the hosting region in West Virginia. In the inaugural year, 36 teams turned out. As word spread, the number of teams soared to 500 in following years, with more than 10,000 more people coming just to watch.

Canaan, which later moved to Snowshoe, West Virginia, was an instant success. Before long, Knight and his company, Granny Gear Productions, added new venues across the country. Other race promoters followed suit, making 24-hour racing the fastest-growing race format. The appeal lay in the casual party atmosphere. Though some pros showed up, most racers were lifestyle cyclists who just wanted to ride hard, camp out, and have fun.

Racers often came in costume, donning bunny ears or disco suits. Venues provided ample food and festivities for the spectators. The race itself was a backdrop for a greater party at large.

Today, even as professional mountain-bike racing ebbs and flows in popularity, 24-hour racing remains enormously successful. There are nearly 20 large-scale races across the country and more small events held by local bike clubs and ski resorts. For long-time riders, these events are an annual tradition. For novices, they're a rite of passage. And for everyone who loves the sport, they're just a roaring good time.

Part Le Mans, *part Woodstock, a 24-hour race is for anyone with a bike and a little Evel Knievel inside.*

OH, YEAH, THE OUTDOORS

As important a role that technology played in defining the history of the mountain bike, it is the places to ride that make the whole endeavor worthwhile.

From Moab to Mt. Snow, Durango to Vancouver, Lake Garda to the Roc d'Azur, the ride is the take-home benefit most worth savoring. Whether you're catching air in the Rockies, splashing through a creek in Costa Rica, or losing some skin on a pineapple-laden trail in Hawaii, riding your bike offroad is what makes the mountain-bike experience complete.

Virtually none of the breakthroughs in frame or suspension technology would mean a thing if there weren't so many fabulous places to put them to use. Far and away, the inherent challenge of the trails is the experience that we live for. And it's that challenge that far outshines the greatness of anything designed on a computer or marketed in a conference room. Long before full-suspension bikes with lightweight carbon-fiber frames and brakes ever showed up at the Slickrock Trail in Moab, the trails were already providing the more rugged a wonderful off-road experience.

The big outdoors *is within reach with a mountain bike.*

TO THE RESCUE

Unfortunately, the very essence of the sport is also the very thing that nearly doomed it. It didn't take long for enthusiastic mountain bikers to come into conflict with other, more traditional user groups out on the trails. Run-ins with hikers, equestrians, and conservationists would soon become the most serious threat to the sport's growth and popularity.

Luckily, a network of trail advocates, not unlike the cottage industry of designers and manufacturers who were responsible for so much of the sport's technological growth, came to the forefront of the land-access battle, which loomed large and threatening in the off-road world.

With trail use *at an all-time high, conflicts between user groups continue to escalate.*

Horse or bike? *Who has the right-of-way?*

In the same tireless fashion that Geoff Ringlé worked a CNC machine to create a fancy new hub, the trail advocates were making phone calls, writing letters, and showing up at city hall meetings. Fortunately for all of us, where the hardware makers could work hard and still turn out a crappy product, there was never a time when the result of an advocate's effort was seen in a bad light.

The biggest drag about trail advocacy is that it just plain isn't inspiring to think about. Licking envelopes could never be as much fun as railing some singletrack! But for the sport to survive, it had to be done, and thankfully, individuals such as Don Douglass and Gibson Anderson, the two men credited with forming the International Mountain Bicycling Association (IMBA), took an early lead in the effort. While the IMBA would eventually go on to capture the attention of both the bike industry and politicians, who too often control our fate, the land-access battle has largely been victorious due to the continued efforts of thousands of committed individuals throughout the world. Civic-minded individuals such as Dwain Abramowski in Michigan, Alan Armstrong in California, and Michael Smith in New York City can be credited as leaders in the pursuit of building and protecting trails. Specialized was one of only a handful of bike companies who shared this vision before the movement went mainstream. Their "Peace on Dirt" campaign was just the sort of positive PR that mountain biking needed to take an early foothold in the land-access crisis.

IMBA cofounder *Don Douglass* (far left) *and Alan Armstrong* (left)

Freeriders *like these guys often catch the brunt of the blows from user groups that oppose mountain biking.*

"We were a tribe,

young and ecstatic,

and at that moment,

the world was ours"

ZAPATA ESPINOSA

Trail Head, *Mountain Bike*, December 2001

INMATES IN CHARGE:
HOW THE INDUSTRY EVOLVED

The year was 1990, and in a quiet corner of southwest Colorado, the town of Durango held the first ever International Cycling Union (UCI)–sanctioned world mountain-bike championships. The rainbow jersey, coveted by the road racers for decades, would now be awarded to both cross-country and downhill dirt bikers. We had arrived!

This race would prove to be a watershed in the sport's cultural history, not unlike when suspension was introduced. Durango not only marked the birth of the sport on a global basis, but it also heralded the arrival of the racer and bike company as celebrities.

Mountain Biking's "Cooperstown" (left),
a long-range goal for any top racer

Organized races had been held for the previous decade, but it wasn't until Durango that athletes and specific products attained cult status. Riders like Ned Overend, Greg Herbold, and Juli Furtado and manufacturers such as Yeti Cycles, Manitou, and Onza were now icons of a sport soon to burst from its mountain origins.

One of the top *professionals to make Durango, Colorado, his home, Myles Rockwell was downhill world champion in 2000.*

By the age of 26, *French rider Anne-Caroline Chausson had a dozen downhill and slalom world championships to her credit.*

JULI FURTADO

An Overnight Sensation

"The slower you go, the more likely it is you'll crash," was Juli Furtado's motto. One of the mountain biking's most ferocious competitors, Furtado bolted from obscurity to dominance in a sport she claimed to have tried just because the "guys were cute."

In reality it was two bum knees that drove her to the bike. After earning a spot on the 1982 U.S. Ski Team at just 15, she pushed too hard and blew out both hinges, leading to a forced retirement at 21. As the saying goes, if you can't walk, you can bike; so, Furtado muscled her way into road cycling and became an instant success—snatching the national championship in 1989. The following year she returned to the ski resorts, only this time atop a mountain bike.

Furtado was an unstoppable force on the mountain-bike circuit—crushing the field her first year as a pro, winning the 1990 cross-country championships. Three years later, she made cycling history capturing the top podium spot in 17 consecutive national and international races. She was a five-time national champion; three-time World Cup champ, and even won downhill championships one year. In 1996, she realized her dream of making the Olympics in mountain biking's debut year.

Sadly, Furtado's remarkable run ended almost as abruptly as it began. In late 1997, after a season plagued by fatigue, ill health, and misdiagnosis, Furtado learned she had systemic lupus, an autoimmune disease that causes pain and inflammation. Her racing career was over. Today, Furtado lives on in the sport through her own line of women-specific mountain bikes.

VITAL STATS

NATIONALITY: American

DATE OF BIRTH: April 14, 1967

CAREER VICTORY HIGHLIGHTS: World Downhill Championships: 1992; National Championships: 1991, 1992, 1993, 1994, 1995; World Cross-Country Championships: 1990; U.S. National Road Championships: 1989

248

When the world championships visited Italy the following year, race results spoke as much about an athlete's personal abilities as about the equipment they used. The battle for territory in the mountain-bike market was raging at full force and everyone wanted in. Who'd have ever envisioned road-racing marques like Colnago and Campagnolo on the winners' podium for a mountain-bike race? It would only get crazier.

By the mid-90s, the mountain-bike industry found itself on a full-fledged rocket propelled into the stratosphere. Mountain-bike–specific magazines had evolved on every continent. The sport had its own hall of fame, established in 1988 in Crested Butte, Colorado. And in 1996, cross-country mountain biking skipped the demonstration status of most young sports and qualified for a permanent place in the Olympics.

Miguel Martinez *hoists his bike as he wins the cross-country race at the 2000 Sydney games.*

TOO BIG TO BE POPULAR

Unfortunately, as the mountain-bike rocketship made its turn into the late '90s, the fuel provided by events such as our Olympic inclusion and Madison Avenue success would prove more flammable than energizing.

We'd grown so large, so quickly, that we seemed to have forgotten who we were, what we were doing, and why we were doing it. Following the 1996 Olympics, the big business fracas—battles over athlete endorsements and the "best bike"—that had enveloped the mountain-bike industry started to take its toll. All the mighty CEO muckety-mucks who invaded the sport when companies were showing big profits and going public were now—when they weren't getting kicked out—scrambling to get out. Corporate credentials were suddenly as unfashionable as the 3-D violet skewers left over from the early days.

Even from the *earliest days,*
corporate sponsorship was key to the
existence of high-level racing.

In our haste to go big, we'd forgotten that the sport's earliest success was brought about by a bunch of passionate bike freaks. The suits-and-ties that came in midterm were, for the most part, not in for the right reason. Sure, some of them may have learned to ride with clipless pedals, but they weren't close to the sport. They couldn't understand the value of bagging peaks in Crested Butte or that the experience was far more valuable than a hefty stock option. They weren't like Joe Breeze who saw the bicycle as not just another SKU (stock-keeping unit) but a type of salvation for mankind. They'd retreat from the races midday for cocktails or a game of golf while Mert Lawwill and Steve "Gravy" Gravenites would be hanging out in the pits late into the night trying to improve the product.

By the late 1990s, at least a quarter of the companies that came along for the ride were suddenly gone. While each loss had its own reasons, it seemed to the casual observer simply that too many companies were run by a bunch of cycling zealots who, while qualified as enthusiasts, proved less so as entrepreneurs. The simplest equation was that too many of the small guys had staked a claim based more on their technical know-how and ingenuity than on sound business skills. However, even though there was a large number of small guys who went away, they could perhaps find some solace in the fact that in the decade that saw the sport's biggest growth, big-time companies like GT and Schwinn also somehow found themselves bankrupt—Schwinn twice! In the end, we all came to realize that more than just youthful enthusiasm and a sheer love of the sport were needed to sustain the business side of things.

While it did *bring money to the sport, corporate sponsorship exacted a high price.*

Rolling along the Riviera

The official mountain-bike season typically wraps up by the end of summer, with many pros hanging up their wheels for the month of October before launching into off-season training. Some, however, make sure they have juice left in the tank for one of the biggest mountain-bike race festivals in Europe—the Roc d'Azur, a French classic that attracts the sport's most elite riders, as well as 10,000 other participants and more than 100,000 spectators to the Frejus beach station along the French Riviera.

Created more than 15 years ago, the Roc d'Azur is held over a four-day period in mid-October each year. At the heart of it is the Roc d'Azur race, a 34-mile loop renowned for its breathtaking beauty as well as for its harsh technical terrain. The course sweeps through the forest on singletrack and sends racers along the border of the Mediterranean Sea,

including a rough, traditional passage on the beach where throngs of spectators spend the day cheering. Along with the elite race, the Roc d'Azur offers something for riders of all ages and abilities. For those who prefer to take the trails at their own pace, there's the Rando Roc, an untimed ramble to the cross-

country race closing ceremony. Amateur riders can tackle a shorter 22-mile course. And there's even a kids' mini race.

Along with the racing, riders and fans can check out BMX exhibitions, special events, such as dances, and the largest French trade fair for cyclists. The event has grown so popular that it has become a tourist destination, with cycling enthusiasts booking vacations that include regional tours, meals, training rides, and, of course, the race itself. Cyclists also are free to come ride the Roc d'Azur all season, though most would agree it's more fun when a few thousand enthusiasts are along for the ride.

The Roc d'Azur *sees as many as 10,000 racers sprint up the beach and rip through the mountains.*

THE NEW SAVIOR—
SAME AS THE OLD

Two years ago when *Mountain Bike* magazine was counting down the 15 most significant people in the sport, we didn't give the nod to some elite racer, rocket scientist, or corporate bigwig, but instead, to an old coot by the name of Victor Vincente of America (VVofA). Having never heard of him, many people in the industry expressed shock over our choice. With all that the mountain-bike industry had accomplished over the years, how was it, they wondered, that we could laud someone with virtually no commercial or even social ties to the inside realm?

Precisely. VVofA, without a doubt, remains emblematic of the sport's roots that we felt necessary to get back to. Though the paradigm of mountain biking had shifted an untold number of times in the previous decade, it seems to be honing in on a semblance of what many thought it was originally. *(continued on page 258)*

(continued on page 258)

"*Vincente is #1 in our book because from the beginning he's pursued poetry, not patents... He's gentle and freakish and wears his iconclasm proud—which is the way a mountain biking forefather should go*"

MOUNTAIN BIKE

January 2001

They might have numbers on their chest, but the simple joy of being out there makes mountain biking the greatest way to spend a day in the outdoors.

While it's doubtful that many people enjoying the current mood swing were actually around "back in the day," the shift is telling in terms of what they want their mountain-bike experience to be. Probably the most significant boost to the "back to the roots" movement was the ascendancy of the 24-hour racing scene that brought a sense of camaraderie and carefree attitude that many felt was lost over the years.

Sure, technological advances continue at a rapid pace, but following all the technology battles, the buyouts, and the infighting, it seems that the sport of mountain biking has finally calmed down long enough to look in the mirror and see its true reflection—passion about having fun. And appreciating the great outdoors. Curiously, one of the sport's best attributes—its sense of smallness and community—seems to have worked against it

because too often the sport was defined by the industry. Many enthusiasts felt trapped by the commercial side of things, which never had anything to do with enjoying fantastic views from the Slickrock Trail loop in Moab or the Mediterranean Sea along the French Riviera. Whatever deals were made at the trade show in Taiwan had no bearing on the ability of a person to go out and enjoy a ride in Copper Canyon.

By the year 2003, the sport seems to be back on track. Though the industry is still bent over, catching its breath from the last decade, it does so with an eye toward the future, and hopefully, an eye toward doing things differently. While traditional racing continues at its roller-coaster pace, the new style of adventure and extreme races is taking hold.

What hasn't changed is the lure that has always made mountain biking so attractive in the first place. The primal impulse is felt by everyone who craves being outdoors. They're looking for adventure and the opportunity to get outside and have fun with their friends and family. The mountain bike remains the perfect vehicle for such pursuits because the mountains themselves provide the perfect reason to start pedaling.

Shredding *the Slickrock Trail near Moab, Utah, is a fat-tire rite of passage.*

CHAPTER 6

THE
GREATEST
RACE

By James Startt

THE FIRST TOUR

A simple business lunch was all it took for two men to conceive of what would become the world's greatest bike race, or at least that's what history shows. In an old-world Paris brasserie called the Zimmer, Geo Lefèvre and Henri Desgrange concocted the idea of a "Tour de France Cycliste." The year was 1902.

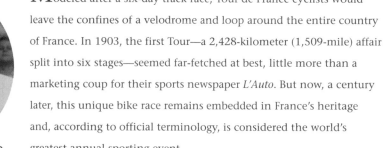

Modeled after a six-day track race, Tour de France cyclists would leave the confines of a velodrome and loop around the entire country of France. In 1903, the first Tour—a 2,428-kilometer (1,509-mile) affair split into six stages—seemed far-fetched at best, little more than a marketing coup for their sports newspaper *L'Auto*. But now, a century later, this unique bike race remains embedded in France's heritage and, according to official terminology, is considered the world's greatest annual sporting event.

Henri Desgrange

The first *Tour de France in 1903 was somewhat more informal than today's race.*

Cycling a century ago was, at best, a fledgling sport, centered first on the bicycle's efficiency as a mode of transportation. Races were largely confined to specially constructed velodromes. But at the end of the 19th century, the idea of racing on roads was growing. Participation also grew, attracting unexpected fans and competitors.

Late-19th-century painter Henri de Toulouse-Lautrec was an avid fan, and Fauvist painter Maurice de Vlaminck reportedly rode the mythic Paris-to-Roubaix race. Cycling reviews in magazines such as *Velo* and *L'Auto* posted average sales of around 25,000— healthy circulation rate even by today's standards. Each new race tried to outdo previous ones. Paris to Rouen was outdone by Bordeaux to Paris, a 400-mile night-and-day affair. And then there was the seemingly endless 745-mile Paris to Brest to Paris, where cyclists ventured from the French capital to the northwestern coastal town and back. The Tour de France idea, however, was unthinkable—at least until Lefevre and Desgrange thought of it. But the idea quickly grew and when they officially announced the race in January of 1903, many considered it unimaginable. *(continued on page 270)*

During its first century *the Tour de France developed its own mythology, one that includes five-time winner American Lance Armstrong* (on poster on lower left).

Although he died *two years before the inaugural Tour de France, French expressionist Henri de Toulouse-Lautrec was fascinated with the bicycle.*

The May Feast

Perhaps nowhere on the planet are people as passionate about cycling as in Italy—home of cycling greats such as the legend Fausto Coppi and the lion king Mario Cipollini, bike frames such as Pinarello and Calnago that rival works of art, and the rolling spectacle that brings it all together with 43 million rabid Italian cycling fans, the Giro d'Italia.

Once deemed the "May Feast" by poetic cyclist Bruno Raschi, the Giro is a treat for the senses. Like the Tour de France, it is an annual three-week stage race that features flat, sprinting stages, time trials, and impossibly high, grueling mountain passes. Though the course changes year to year, it always promises challenge and opportunity for racers of all specialties and generally covers more than 2,000 miles before ending in Milan. The Italian tour also features prerace hoopla including at least 1,000 vehicles representing the media, cycling teams, technical assistance, and of course, the parade of advertisers tossing candy and trinkets to onlookers along the course. Unlike the Tour, the Giro is considered accessible to the everyday fan. The entourage is considerably smaller, allowing cycling enthusiasts to get an up-close and personal view of their favorite competitors. And it's not uncommon for top riders to even be available for pictures and autographs.

Some even consider the Giro d'Italia more exciting than the Tour de France in that the field is wide open. Though there are always a few prerace favorites, almost any strong candidate can, and often does, take the top podium spot. Combine the ever-exciting racing with fervent fans and bright spring weather with a backdrop of superb food and great wine, and it's easy to understand how this 87-year-old event will likely be popular for centuries to come.

The Giro is to Italy what the Tour is to France.

After all, in 1899, a Tour de France automobile race was already considered quite a feat, and the average speed of 30 miles per hour was impressive. But to tackle the same circuit on a bicycle! No one in those days, of course, ever could have imagined that a century later bicycle racers would loop around the country at nearly the same speeds as those early automobiles.

Those crazy enough to sign up for the inaugural run were, well, a strange breed—a cross between circus *saltimbanques* and horse-racing jockeys. The analogy to equestrian sports does not simply come from the fact that participants wore brightly colored, skin-tight outfits, but also because they spoke a mysterious, insider language specifically adapted to the intricacies of their sport. And, as in horse racing, the mystery often continued into the arena of competition, as unspoken arrangements between competitors were commonplace. In 1904, the Tour was almost abolished due to widespread cheating.

The first-ever Tour *was part publicity stunt, part cannonball run.*

Participants in early Tours *resembled crosses between circus act performers and horse-racing jockeys with individual styles and racing antics.*

In down moments, however, the circus spirit took over. Early Tour cyclists could be seen standing on their hands on chairs or demonstrating two-wheeled acrobatics. Of course, any of the 60 riders starting the 1903 Tour on a fixed-gear bike weighing in at more than 30 pounds had to be a little off his rocker. But history can thank them, especially the 21 who finished. They created the mold, one that included an unimaginable appetite for suffering and hard physical labor that remains the essence of any aspiring bicycle racer today.

From its early years *through today, the Tour de France draws men with an insatiable appetite for suffering.*

Earlier *in the Tour's history, riders rode for national teams and were responsible for the maintenance on their equipment— hence the spare tires twisted around their shoulders.*

THE MAKINGS OF THE GREATEST RACE

In the early years, the race organizers concerned themselves with establishing their event and giving it lasting guidelines. Additional kilometers would be added (the race is now 3,350 kilometers, or about 2,082 miles), not to mention the mythic mountains. But while the first Tours resembled spectacle as much as they did pure sport, organizers soon became increasingly interested in the sporting aspects of the event. As years went by, other events like the time trial and team time trial were added.

Extracurricular events such the ever-popular circuslike publicity caravan that rolls in front of the race also have been added to entertain spectators waiting for the race to pass them. And in recent years, elements such as the VIP start village have grown. But throughout the generations, race organizers have maintained that improving the sporting aspects of the race is the common denominator to any change. Current race director Jean-Marie Leblanc insists that, "it is our job to make the race even so that a climber has as much chance as a time trialer."

With his comeback *from cancer, American Lance Armstrong* (seen here in the 2001 edition) *has bolstered global interest in the Tour de France.*

Jean-Marie Leblanc

In an effort to connect all of France's major cities, the inaugural Tour was divided into six individual stages: Paris to Lyon, Lyon to Marseille, Marseille to Toulouse, Toulouse to Bordeaux, Bordeaux to Nantes, and Nantes to Paris. Stages averaged 250 miles in length and were followed by several rest days. Riders tackled their first mountain, the modest Ballon d'Alsace, in 1905. But when the race ventured into the Pyrenees Mountains in 1910, riders called the race organizers "assassins." Forced to push and pedal their way up virtual cow paths, their cries were not unwarranted. But such hardships and the exploits that ensued soon became part of the Tour legend.

The Tour de France, *seen here in 1938, has always had an intensely romantic image with the general public.*

Riders *of the mid-century Tours battled it out on the same demanding mountain passes as today's riders.*

In 1969, a Tour rookie named Eddy Merckx unveiled his immense strength when he waltzed away from his competitors on the famed Tourmalet climb in the Pyrenees, setting off on a epic 90-mile solo ride that left his nearest competitor 8 minutes behind. "What this sublime cyclist did," wrote then race director Jacques Goddet, "had never yet been written in the annals of the road." In 1975, six years and five Tour victories later, the same Merckx, withered and worn by the years of intense racing, wilted on the climb to Pra-Loup in the Alps. It would be his last day in yellow.

The Tour de France (left) *passed through stunning Alpine scenery.*

Merckx *has more stage wins and more days in yellow than any other man to ride the Tour.*

Spain's Miguel
Indurain *was the
first-ever rider to
win five consecutive
Tour de France races.*

In 1986, the legendary Alpe d'Huez was
the stage for the historic transfer of power
between two teammates, five-time defending
champion Bernard Hinault of France and his
protégé, American Greg LeMond. LeMond,
in yellow, rode together with Hinault before
handing his one-time master the stage
victory. In 1991, Spaniard Miguel Indurain
forced LeMond's own demise on the Val-
Louron climb in the Pyrenees. But five years
later Big Mig's own reign came to an end
in the Alps when he wilted on the climb to
Les Arcs.

Frenchman Bernard Hinault *had an iron grip
on the Tour in the late '70s and early '80s. Today
he helps to organize the race.*

MIGUEL INDURAIN
A Humble Hero

Awed by his seemingly effortless string of stunning victories, his contemporaries deemed him "the Alien," "the Motorcycle," and "Big Miguel." Though he was one of the most feared men in the pelotons of the 1990s, Miguel Indurain was defined as much by his humility and grace as his power and prowess.

A natural athlete, Indurain won the second road race he entered at the tender age of 12. He spent his teens tearing up the Spanish circuit and in 1985, at age 20, he was signed to his first professional team. Victories proved more elusive as a pro, however, and Indurain spent five years as one of many strong, yet unremarkable European racers. Undaunted, he simply continued racing . . . and improving, eventually winning a few prestigious races and capturing two Tour de France stage wins.

It finally all came together for Indurain in 1991, when he captured his first Tour de France victory. The following four years and five total consecutive Tour de France victories would establish Indurain as a legend of the sport, a label he graciously declined. "You cannot compare me to them," he said of the dominant racers such as Eddy Merckx and Bernard Hinault to whom he was being compared. "I just want to be Indurain."

Today fans and fellow racers remember Indurain as much for the races he didn't win as for those he did. More than once, he ceded a sure win to a racer he deemed deserving of that day's top honors—a gentlemanly feat that will not soon be surpassed.

VITAL STATS

NATIONALITY: Spanish

DATE OF BIRTH: July 16, 1964

CAREER VICTORY HIGHLIGHTS: Tour de France: 1991, 1992, 1993, 1994, 1995; Giro d'Italia: 1992, 1993; Olympic Time Trial: 1996, 1993; World Cup Classic (*Clasica San Sebastien*): 1990

And, of course, American superhero Lance Armstrong has habitually used historic climbs such as Sestrières, Alpe d'Huez, or Hautacam to construct each of his five Tour victories. To date, none have proved to be his demise.

Armstrong *has written a novel's worth of heroic exploits in the Tour.*

Certainly today, despite the century-old cries of "assassin," the Tour is quite simply unthinkable without its legendary mountains. But Tour directors never limited their innovations to altitude. In an effort to add suspense, race organizers in the 1920s transformed flat stages into a sort of team time trial, where each team rode together, trying to post the best time. This formula, however, quickly proved flawed as it gave riders on strong teams an unfair advantage. In 1934, they introduced the first individual time trial, a 51.5-mile timed stretch from La Roche-sur-Yon to Nantes. While it proved to be the demise of race hero René Vietto, one of the race's first king of the mountains, organizers considered it a success as it offered nonclimbers a chance to make their mark. And today, time trialing is an integral part of every Tour.

Two burly riders *shake hands before a 1934 time trial.*

The New Proving Ground

The third and final great three-week tour in Europe is the Vuelta a España, held each year in September, following the Giro d'Italia and the Tour de France. Though the Spanish tour is younger than the other two, not quite 60 years old, and somewhat less esteemed than the prized Italian and French events, the Vuelta is quickly becoming where to catch cycling's newest rising stars.

Like the other major tours, the Vuelta alters its route slightly each year in an attempt to keep the venue interesting and offer unique challenges to racers in every discipline. Climbers, in particular, can make their mark here, with legendary climbs such as El Angliru, a mountain so vertical that racers say it makes other classic mountain passes feel like "child's play" in comparison. Though the Vuelta tends to be relatively short, spanning fewer than 2,000 miles, its numerous mountaintop finishes, time trials, and sprinting stages make the Vuelta similar to the Tour de France in the mental and physical energy it takes to complete it. For that reason, up-and-coming pros use the Vuelta to show off their form and attract media and sponsor

attention. It is often said that if you can win the Vuelta, you're in the limelight for the Tour.

Even established pros have used the Vuelta as a proving ground. In 1999, German sensation Jan Ullrich dominated the Spanish tour as proof that after two years of problems and defeats, he was back in form. And in 1998, just two years after his stunning cancer disclosure, Lance Armstrong roared into the Vuelta, finishing an impressive fourth place, as a sign that he could (and would) win the following year's Tour de France. The Vuelta may never get any bigger, but it certainly will not shrink in importance anytime soon.

Wearing the leader's jersey *in the tour of Spain* (left) *can be a precursor to Tour de France glory.*
Spain's national tour (right) *is as much a postcard for that country as the Tour is for France.*

THE MAGICAL
MYSTERY OF THE TOUR

What makes the Tour so special is not simply its magnificent, truly unmatched sporting exploits, but also the relationship it has with its people. "The Tour de France," says current Tour chief Leblanc, "is an uncommon human adventure, an unequaled cycling race, but also an incredible popular and social event."

The Tour de France succeeds in surpassing any other sporting event—the Super Bowl, world cups, the World Series, and the Olympics included—for one simple reason: It takes sport outside of the stadium. For three weeks every July, the small country roads of France become a nonstop stadium, lined with fans from around the world, who all manage to impose a certain carnival spirit on what remains a sporting event of the highest level. On these roads, fans

For the millions *of spectators* (below) *who watch the Tour every year, it's an incredible (and free) experience.* **As Armstrong (right) has tamed** *his Texas accent, French fans have started to embrace him as their own.*

commune with their heroes as racers often pass within arm's length. It is not uncommon for fans to hand riders water bottles. Even an encouraging push to a lagging rider is overlooked. Race organizers ignore such details because they know that fans never push favored riders, for it is understood among the millions of fans that they should never affect the race between the favorites.

"France is a magical place for such a race," says three-time winner LeMond, ever popular in the land of the Tour. "Everything comes together for the Tour. They close the country down for you. The roads take on their own identity. There is a romance to them and they belong to the Tour. You couldn't have this race in any other country."

Even the main street *in Paris shuts down when the Tour comes to town.*

HEROS OF THE TOUR

In an almost uncanny fashion, each generation of Tour riders has produced their own breed of champion. From the carnivalesque Lucien Petit-Breton, winner of the Tour in 1907 and 1908, to the cannibalesque Eddy Merckx, winner of five Tours in the 1960s and 1970s, to the ironlike American Lance Armstrong, winner of the past five races—the great Tour champions all seem to somehow embody their age.

Fittingly, the race's first champion, Maurice Garin, symbolically sported a handle-bar moustache, which was fashionable in the European fin de siècle spirit and even more so for a bicycle racer. In 1908, the modest Petit-Breton became the first two-time winner of the Tour.

Maurice Garin, *the first winner of the Tour, looks back to check the competition.*

Much of his notoriety, however, didn't come from the fact that he won the race twice, but that he rode as an independent on a makeshift bicycle, yet beat better-organized, more powerful riders and teams. His victories embodied the pioneering spirit of the Tour's first golden age. In 1920, Belgium's Philippe Thys became the first three-time winner. Noted for his marathon training rides, his hard-work ethic gave hope to a generation recovering from the ruins of World War I.

Italian Gino Bartali *is one of the great characters to win the Tour de France (in 1938 and 1948).*

Italy's Gino Bartali did the same in 1948, when he won the Tour for a second time, 10 years after his first victory. Although he lost the golden years of his own career to World War II, his second victory showed a world that certain things could be as before.

He would be replaced in 1949 by his countryman Fausto Coppi, considered by many to be the first modern-day champion for his ability to incorporate specialized diet and training to the sport.

His compatriot, *Fausto Coppi, was the classiest champion to ever win the lap of France.*

JACQUES ANQUETIL
The Unconventional Champion

In a sport that prides itself on unwritten rules and codes of ethics, French sensation Jacques Anquetil was an aristocratic outlaw. From his unconventional form—toes pointed to the ground, arms and legs stretched like a spider—to his tactics—exert only enough to win—to his air of arrogance, "Anq" was not a popular "favorite." Yet, his prowess during his 19-year reign was undeniable.

Anquetil rode himself into the top echelon of cycling dignitaries largely through his tremendous time-trialing abilities. He would simply hang close to his rivals for days on end, then blow them off the pavement on time-trial days—an approach that earned him five Tour de France victories. Though this measured strategy didn't win over fans, it did earn him remarkable achievements. He was one of only two riders to win the Giro d'Italia and Tour de France in the same year. And in a seemingly superhuman feat, he won the 1965 Dauphiné to Libéré, a grueling week-long Alpine stage race, then flew to the western coast of France, slept four hours, and rode off to victory in a rainy, dark 365-mile Bordeaux-to-Paris race.

Ultimately, it wasn't his myriad podium finishes as much as his ability to suffer on the bike that earned Anquetil admirers. From smashing into a telephone pole at the completion of a grueling, yet victorious, two-man time trial in 1962 to his talent for mashing enormous gears over monster climbs, Anquetil left little doubt of his unparalleled capabilities. Yet today, he remains one of the least appreciated champions of the sport.

> ### VITAL STATS
>
> **NATIONALITY:** French
>
> **DATE OF BIRTH:** January 8, 1934
>
> **CAREER VICTORY HIGHLIGHTS:** Tour de France: 1957, 1961, 1962, 1963, 1964; Giro d'Italia: 1960, 1964; Ghent–Wevelgem: 1964; Vuelta a España: 1963

Anquetil was the first rider *to win five Tours. Yet his old form and arrogant demeanor hurt his popularity with the public.*

Three-time winner Louison Bobet (1953, 1954, 1955) embodied the popular rebirth of the Tour after World War II, while his countryman Jacques Anquetil, the race's first five-time winner (1957, 1961, 1962, 1963, 1964) was as famous for his playboy lifestyle in the swinging '60s as he was for his overwhelming exploits on the bike. Belgium's Eddy Merckx dominated the race in the late 1960s and early 1970s. While his long Elvis-like sideburns were perhaps slightly behind post-Beatlemania times, he matched contemporary champions like Mohammad Ali with his insatiable appetite for winning, justifiably earning the nickname "the Cannibal."

France's Bernard Hinault brought the race back home by winning it five times between 1978 and 1985, but his successor American Greg LeMond symbolized the growing internationalism of the race when he won it three times between 1986 and 1990.

In the years
after World War II,
Louison Bobet was just
the kind of hero
France needed.

Five-time winner Miguel Indurain mirrored an age of increased specialization, focusing his energies only on the Tour during the 1990s. And then, of course, there is today's overwhelming champion, Lance Armstrong, who beat life-threatening cancer to become the top Tour rider of his generation. His ability to beat cancer as well as his ability to go on to compete are successes for modern medicine and technology. A meticulous champion with an insatiable appetite for suffering, Armstrong ignores no details in his training, diet, or high-tech equipment.

Julio Jimenez (left) *winning stage 16 of the Tour in 1966*
Like Hinault before him, *Armstrong* (right) *is a master time-trial rider and tactician.*

But the Tour is as much about its many countless losers as it is about its celebrated winners. Eugène Christophe was the first rider to wear the famed yellow jersey when it was introduced midway through the 1919 race so that organizers and spectators could better discern the leader. Yet Christophe never won the race and lost two Tours in 1913 and 1919, when he broke his fork. In 1934, neophyte René Vietto won the public's heart but lost the Tour when he gave his front wheel to his teammate Antonin Magne, the eventual winner. His generosity symbolized the team spirit in this originally individual sport. In the 1960s, Raymond Poulidor continually came up short in the face of iron-man Jacques Anquetil, and in the 1970s, he fell behind Eddy Merckx. While "Pou Pou" never wore the yellow jersey for a single day, he always seemed to win the popularity contest.

Although he never won *the Tour or even wore the leader's jersey, Polidor is still loved as a champion in France.*

SMOOTH LEGS

A Time-Honored Tradition

Peek below the surface of any rough and tumble professional peloton and you'll notice a strangely soft underside—shaved legs. Though shearing one's legs baby-bottom smooth has long been considered decidedly feminine, cyclists worldwide have adopted the practice as a symbol of a rider's commitment to the sport.

No one's really sure where the tradition got started, or why, but there's plenty of speculation. Better aerodynamics is one of the most common explanations given for choosing hairless gams. But even the most hard-core cyclists freely admit that the 1,000th of a second that they save on wind resistance is hardly a deciding factor. More logical are the claims that shaved legs are easier to clean and they heal more quickly after a crash. Since many cyclists also frequent massage therapists to flush their muscles and

speed recovery, having smooth, hairless quads and calves allows for a more fluid rubdown, free of painful, awkward hair yanking.

Then there's the vanity factor. Reasonable explanations aside, some cyclists will admit they shave their legs simply because it makes them look better. Pushing pedals over hundreds of miles creates diamond-cut calves and bulging quadriceps. As any body builder will tell you, those muscles are easier to

admire without a mass of hair in the way. This could explain why some cyclists shave year-round though they may not be anywhere near a bike during the cold winter months.

You certainly don't need to shave your legs to be considered a dedicated cyclist, but if you see a well-muscled man with fuzz-barren legs, you can safely guess he's a member of the club.

Smoothly shaved legs, *one of the great traditions in professional cycling*

303

THE DARK SIDE OF THE TOUR

The mass popularity of the Tour has not come without a price. Since the race's inception, the inherent charm of the Tour has been marred by hype and scandal. Director Leblanc often laments that, "the Tour is a victim of its own success"—a claim that is not unwarranted.

How many sponsorship logos can you count as Miguel Indurain and Claudio Chiappucci ascend an alpine pass?

Business and marketing interests continue to take the spotlight, focusing instead on the show *around* the race. The famed publicity caravan continually lengthens; the marketing and consumer side of the event seemingly never ceases to grow. Today the number of official race vehicles commands disproportionate significance, making it difficult for fans to see the race. And many journalists, who traditionally followed in the race so they could add colorful details to their reports, simply prefer to watch from the press hall rather than fight with VIP cars for a glimpse of the race.

With multinational giants *like Coca-Cola putting their name on the line, the Tour is big business.*

THE GREATEST RACE **305**

And then there is the infamous "D" word. Drugs are the most nagging problem. Since bicycle racing's pioneer years, the sport (with the Tour as its biggest effigy) has been prey to accusations of drugs. And, as witnessed in the notorious Festina Affair in 1998, cycling has never been able to free itself from such sinister vices. Already in 1908, after his second Tour victory, Petit-Breton defended himself against drugging charges in the pages of *L'Auto*, the race's sponsoring newspaper: "It's been said that I owe my principal victories to drugs. Permit me to deny this absurd noise."

But over the years there have been too many proven cases of doping to discount the issue simply as "absurd noise." In 1924, the legendary Pelissier brothers—noted as much for their brutal attacks on the road as for their criticism of Tour organizers—abandoned the race over what they considered to be an unfair ruling. Later that day, they met with journalist Albert Londres in a roadside bar. "You don't have any idea of what the Tour is," said an obviously frustrated Henri. "We suffer from beginning to end. You want to see how we ride? Look. Here is the cocaine for the eyes. Here is the chloroform for the gums. And the pills? You want to see the pills?" After reaching in his sack and grabbing an assortment of pills, his brother Francis added, "In short, we ride on dynamite."

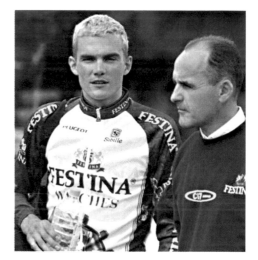

While still popular today, *Richard Virenque was at the center of the 1998 scandal that endangered the existence of the Tour.*

JAN ULLRICH
A Troubled Champion

In 1997, Jan Ullrich was christened the next big thing. In 1996, at only 22, he took second place in the Tour de France and a year later won the grand Tour handily. A notoriously powerful climber and time trialist, the cycling world was at his feet—until the ground beneath them began to crumble.

Ullrich started racing at the tender age of 8 and by 13 was being groomed for a professional career. His youthful dedication paid off when powerhouse team Telekom signed him in 1995. After his Tour de France success in 1997, however, Ullrich became a superstar. Too much celebration and too little training left him about 25 pounds overweight for the 1998 Tour, which he lost to Marco Pantani. A knee injury cut his 1999 season short. Though he scored victories in the Olympics and the World Championships in

the following seasons, he rolled into the 2000 Tour overweight and lost to Lance Armstrong, who beat him again in 2001.

In 2002, a frustrated Ullrich came apart at the seams. Chronic knee problems again forced him from the Tour. Shortly thereafter, he crashed his car in a drunken-driving incident and was later suspended for six months after testing positive for club drugs he took during a night of partying. Though 2003 started positively with Ullrich signing

with Team Coast, team financial problems make his comeback questionable.

Though Ullrich has had success, many feel that injury and especially his off-the-bike behavior have prevented him from reaching his true potential. His second-place finish to Lance Armstrong in the 2003 Tour de France suggests his problems are behind him, and the star is rising again.

VITAL STATS

NATIONALITY: German

DATE OF BIRTH: December 2, 1973

CAREER VICTORY HIGHLIGHTS: Tour de France: 1997; Vuelta a España: 1999; Olympic Road: 2000; German Road Championship: 2001; World Championships Time Trial: 2001

In 1960, French up-and-comer Roger Rivière crashed on a descent in the Pyrenees, paralyzed for life. Amphetamines were found in his jersey pocket. British rider Tom Simpson collapsed and died on Mont Ventoux in the 1967 Tour. Similar substances were found in his body.

And today, even with the rise of sports science that should eliminate the need for doping, the temptation is often too great. Unfortunately, the Festina Affair was likely an indication of a greater problem. Less than a year later, Italy's Marco Pantani, winner of the 1998 Tour, was expelled while leading the neighboring Giro d'Italia when he failed to pass a blood test. Numerous other cases of doping within the sport continue to compromise the efforts of those riders who are clean. And because the Tour is cycling's masthead event, it suffers indirectly from any doping scandal reported within the sport.

Despite such flaws, the Tour—justifiably considered a French national landmark—continues to grow in popularity. Perhaps no century could have been better than the 20th to cradle such a competition. It will be remembered as a century of great innovation when man continually pushed the boundaries of his own limitations. And in no other sporting event have athletes continually pushed their own physical and psychological limits day in and day out.

British rider Tom Simson *collapses near the summit of Mont Ventoux during the 1967 tour. Today a monument marks the spot of his demise.*

Although the Tour becomes increasingly high-tech and the media and marketing hype continue to snowball, there remains a timeless element to the Tour de France, a simple bike race rolling across the landscape of a magnificent country. There is a simple beauty to this event that defies civilization's eternal march toward modernity. It is this endearing aspect of the world's greatest bike race that continues to grab our imagination. Perhaps that is why every man, woman, and child who has seen this race, even for a passing instant, remembers it for a lifetime.

Despite the forces *pulling at the Grande Boucle, its beauty and drama are timeless.*

AFTERWORD

By Joe Lindsey

The trail beckons, crookedly. It drops away beneath you, picking a delicate path among rocks and roots, twisting around trees and grade reversals, before disappearing gradually into the trees. Your front wheel rolls into the first section; the line appears unbidden before you and the bike floats over, rather than through, the rock garden. Your unblinking eyes scan farther down the trail, mentally picking up and storing each section and the means to get through it in your short-term subconscious. Your brain is active, taking in a thousand myriad interpretations and options to plot the right solution but is at the same time perfectly calm, unobstructed by extraneous thought; consciousness only momentarily surfaces amid the bliss of simply riding.

These emotions and experiences transform us, not just as cyclists, but as people. In our everyday lives, cycling helps us in ways we cannot count. We are fitter, healthier people. Riding is a demanding sport, one that opens up a world of healthier habits and lifestyle, of eating well, and of the benefits of exercise. The determination to gut out the last few miles of a century when you're dehydrated and sore, muscles cramping, transfers almost seamlessly to other aspects of life.

Any challenge becomes easier to meet because you have faced and overcome obstacles on the bike.

The act of riding is also solace, meditation. It calms and adds clarity, perspective to the ability to deal with problems. A ride is a mental reset button, a ritual we undertake when we need time for ourselves, time spent doing something purely for the joy of it, in search of the moment when we lose our names and our identities and become simply the act of riding.

When you experience that perfect moment, your heart must sink because you know you can never find it again—it has come and passed and cannot be held on to or even properly remembered; memory would require your conscious self to be present, and it wasn't. But you must still try; you must search for that feeling again and again. It is what it means to ride.

The sensations riding evokes in us—the exhilarating rush of speed that gives us wings, the rawness of morning air drawn into the lungs, the sense of losing self in self—these are all the reasons we ride. We ride because it feels like flying. We ride because it feels like home.

CREDITS

ABOUT THE CONTRIBUTORS

Bill Strickland is the executive editor of *Bicycling* magazine; has ridden and written about the sport of cycling for more than 20 years; raced on the road, on mountain bikes, and in velodromes; published stories in *Men's Health, Men's Journal, Blue, Parenting,* and other national magazines; and commented on cycling for *Good Morning America, The Early Show,* CBS Sports, and ESPN. His books include *The Quotable Cyclist, Mountain Biking: The Ultimate Guide to the Ultimate Ride,* and *On Being a Writer.*

Mark Riedy fell in love with cycling at the age of 13, when shifters were still on the downtube and energy food was a chili cheeseburger at Rudy's near his hometown of Tiffin, Ohio. In the intervening 22 years, he's lived and ridden in New York, Los Angeles, and San Francisco. He's written and worked for *Bicycling* and *Mountain Bike* magazines for nearly a decade and has contributed to *Outside, Popular Science,* and *I.D.* magazines as well as books on cycling and other subjects.

Joe Lindsey has raced and ridden bikes for 15 years and is a contributing writer to *Bicycling* magazine. His work has also appeared in *Outside,, Fodor's Travel Guides, Adventure Sports,* and *5280.* He has written about cycling since graduating from the University of Colorado eight years ago, covering the people, places, events, and culture that make the sport such a fascinating activity.

Nicholas Oddy is a bicycle historian and lecturer in history of design in the historical and critical studies department at Glasgow School of Art. He has presented various talks on the bicycle, most notably "An Invaluable Refinement: The Aesthetic of the Cycle Accessory in the Late 19th and 20th Centuries" at the 1996 International Cycle History Conference held in Buffalo.

Zapata "Zap" Espinoza has worked for *LA Weekly* and *Motocross Action* magazines and was an editor of *Mountain Bike Action* magazine, which under his leadership became the largest mountain-bike publication in the industry. He's spent recent years writing for *Bicycling* and *Mountain Bike* magazines. Espinoza is one of the most visible and colorful figures in mountain-bike journalism. He writes to promote cycling safety, advocacy, and merchandising.

James Startt, admittedly nothing more than pack fodder in the 1992 Olympic trials, has made his greatest contribution to the sport as a journalist and a photographer. Now an avid lunch-time cyclist, Startt, the European correspondent to *Bicyling,* has covered 14 Tours de France and authored *Tour de France/Tour de Force,* the first history of the Tour de France written in English.

Selene Yeager is a certified fitness trainer, avid cyclist, expert-class mountain-bike racer, triathlete, professional writer, and author of *Selene Yeager's Perfectly Fit.* She is a contributing editor at *Prevention* magazine and dishes out training advice monthly as *Bicycling* magazine's "Fitness Chick." Her work has also appeared in *Men's Health, Runner's World, Cosmopolitan, Fitness, Cooking Light,* and *Marie Claire* magazines.

INDEX

Boldfaced page references indicate photographs and captions.